CREATE TO LEARN

DIGITAL SKILLS & TRADITIONAL TEACHINGS FROM FIRST NATIONS, MÉTIS, AND INUIT CREATIVES

Connected North

Canada

TakingITGlobal
117 Peter Street, Suite 212
Toronto, Ontario
M5V 0M3

ISBN: 978-0-578-86731-1 (paperback)
ISBN: 978-0-578-86066-4 (hardback)
ISBN: 978-0-578-88055-6 (ebook)

Produced with the financial support of the Government of Canada's CanCode program

Cover design by Shaikara David, Akwesasne Mohawk Territory

Writing by Alison Tedford, Kwakiutl First Nation

www.createtolearn.ca

This resource is dedicated to the 20,000+ First Nations, Métis and Inuit students we serve through the Connected North program. We hope the skills and knowledge shared in this book will help to inspire new opportunities for you as you embark on your next steps in your creative journey.

We would like to acknowledge the land and the Indigenous artists who have shared their knowledge and teachings in this textbook, along with their ancestors who have offered so much for current and future generations. We are grateful for the opportunity to showcase so many experts from different communities with you in this format. We trust that you will enjoy the gift of having access to the insights shared with great care and respect.

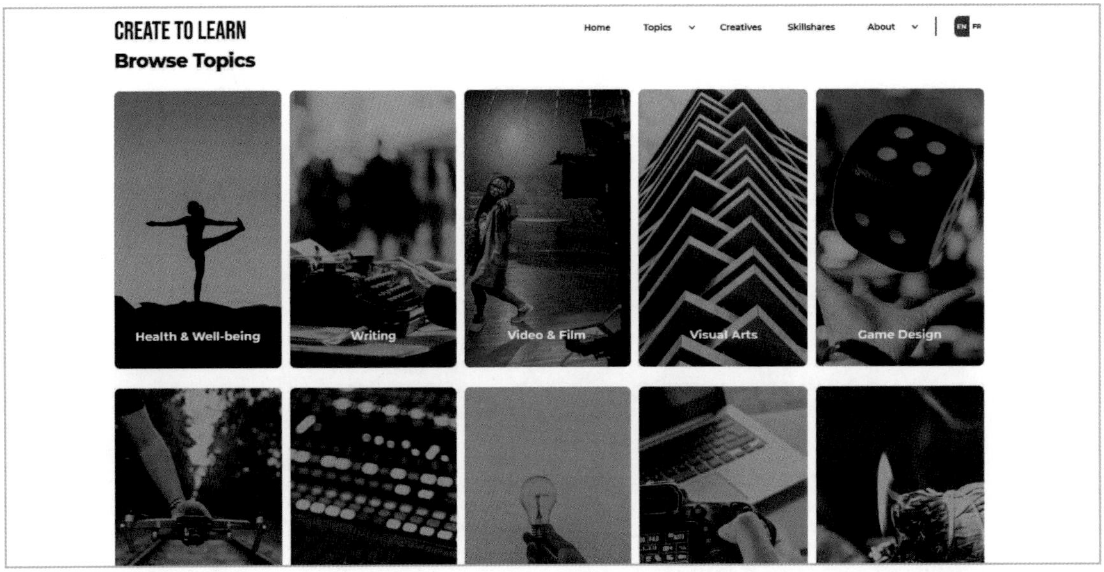

CREATE TO LEARN

Home Topics Creatives Skillshares About | EN FR

Browse Topics

Health & Well-being | Writing | Video & Film | Visual Arts | Game Design

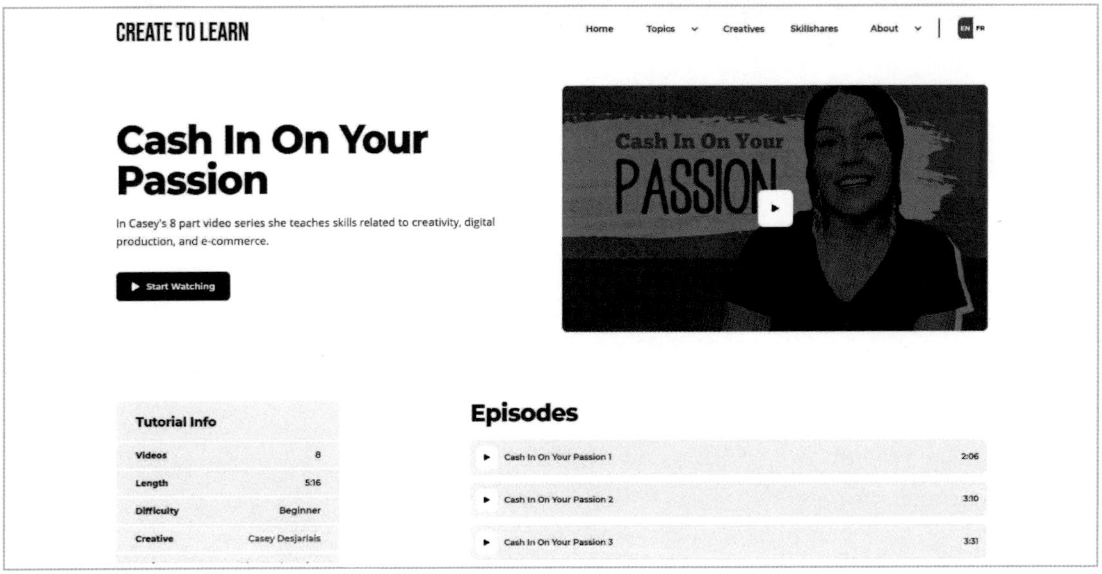

CREATE TO LEARN

Home Topics Creatives Skillshares About | EN FR

Cash In On Your Passion

In Casey's 8 part video series she teaches skills related to creativity, digital production, and e-commerce.

▶ Start Watching

Cash In On Your PASSION

Tutorial Info

Videos	8
Length	5:16
Difficulty	Beginner
Creative	Casey Desjarlais

Episodes

▶ Cash In On Your Passion 1	2:06
▶ Cash In On Your Passion 2	3:10
▶ Cash In On Your Passion 3	3:31

WANT TO TAKE YOUR LEARNING FURTHER?

EXPLORE 50+ TUTORIALS BY FIRST NATIONS, MÉTIS AND INUIT CREATIVES ACROSS THE WEB AND IN OUR MOBILE APPS!

WWW.CREATETOLEARN.CA

CONTENTS

Aaaniin

Ai ᐊᐃ

Boozhoo

Gilakas'la

Kew kew

Kii-te-daas a

Oki

Pjil'asi

Shé:kon

Tân'si

Wa.é ák.wé

Wachayea ᐚᒌᔮ

WE'RE SO EXCITED THAT YOU HAVE THIS BOOK IN YOUR HANDS!

We launched our Create to Learn program in 2017, and it's been an honour to work with youth and students from more than 100 Indigenous communities on building their digital skills to date. Through partnerships with imagineNATIVE, Chiefs of Ontario, Nunavut Sivuniksavut, the Students Commission, Canadian Roots Exchange, and the Inclusive Design Institute, we held in person training with dozens of amazing First Nations, Métis and Inuit creatives as trainers.

When COVID-19 forced school closures and limited travelling, gears started turning in our heads. How could we continue sharing skills with those now learning at home, and how could we provide much-needed work to the creators who were now unable to travel and teach as they had hoped?

We launched Create to Learn@Home, hiring more than 50 creators to develop training videos to share their skills with the world. In the last 9 months, the program has exceeded our expectations, with more than 300 videos attracting over 100,000 views. We've worked to make the videos as accessible as possible - from launching Apple TV, Fire TV and Roku apps for TV users to shipping USB keys pre-loaded with the content to dozens of schools and community partners in the North.

And now, we're pleased to present this book in print to you, featuring these amazing creative talents. We hope you enjoy the skills and knowledge they have to share!

In friendship,

Michael Furdyk
Jennifer Corriero
Dallas Pelly
Jade Roberts
Jayson Moore

The Create to Learn Program Team at TakingITGlobal

CASH IN ON YOUR PASSION

Casey Desjarlais

View the videos in this series online! Scan the QR code, or visit http://www.tigurl.org/cashin

"There is nothing more important to me than spending time at home with my kids, becoming an entrepreneur has allowed me the time to do so."

Casey Desjarlais is a Cree and Anishnaabe mother and business owner from Treaty Four and Treaty Six territories in Saskatoon who created a clothing line called 30604 Apparel, now Sweetgrass Clothing Co with her partner, Dakota Bear. When they first got started, they did everything themselves, from their logo, their marketing materials, website, and promotions. Casey shares that knowledge and experience through her Cash in on Your Passion series.

"As Indigenous people, we are creators. It is in our natural abilities to create."

LESSON 1: THE THREE W'S

Casey shared the three key questions you need to be asking as you create and refine your business idea.

- What product are you selling or what service are you providing?
- Who are you selling your product to, or who is going to be using your service?
- What platform are you going to be selling your product or service on?

Whether you're going to be selling on Etsy, Wix, Shopify, Facebook or Instagram, these are the points you need to consider as you prepare to Cash In On Your Passion, just like Casey did.

LESSON 2: BASICS OF BRANDING

Branding is so important because it builds trust and reliability within your customer and your audiences. It also maintains consistency.

In this lesson, Casey walks us through the things you need to know about creating your brand.

YOUR NAME

The name that you choose for your business should have some significance. Casey chose Sweetgrass Clothing Co because sweetgrass grows abundantly where she is from and it is a sacred medicine. Check to make sure your business name isn't already in use.

YOUR BRAND COLOR

Casey chose the colour pink because her spirit name is Pink Earth Woman. She also picked olive green for sweetgrass and white to bring it all together. The colours you pick should have significance to your business and each will emit different energies so it's important to keep that in mind.They should also be featured on all of your platforms: your website, your social media, your logo and even in your products.

YOUR FONT

Whether you pick cursive, graffiti, bolds, stencils, the font basically builds your business's personality. Make your business and your brand stand out with the right font.

YOUR LOGO

Your colours, your font and your name should all be within your logo. Your logo brings it all together.

LESSON 3: DECOLONIZE BY DESIGN

"Representation is important. When I create my designs, I aim to empower other Indigenous people by representation and by incorporating our tradition and our culture and our values through the designs that I create."

In this lesson, Casey shows you how to create a logo for your work. She uses Canva.com to easily create designs.

1. **Get started**. Go to Canva.com

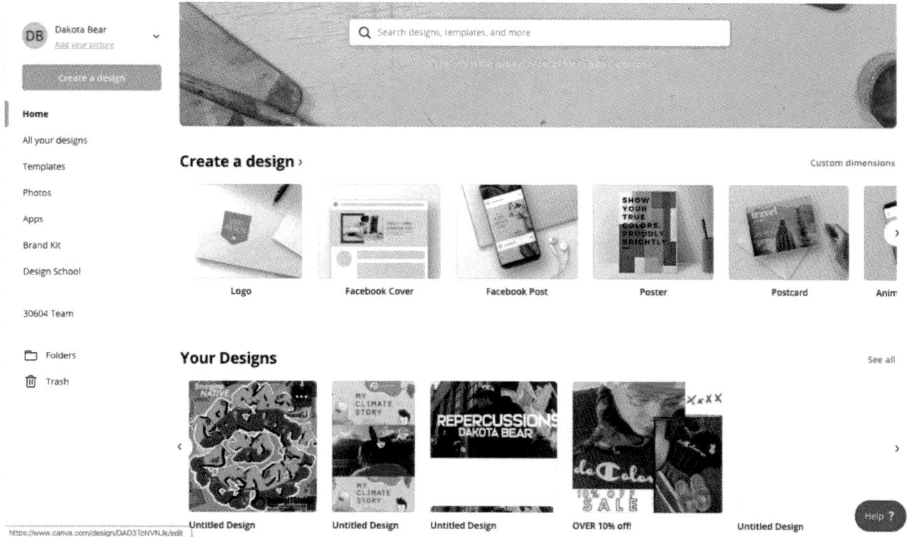

2. **Set your brand kit.** Add your brand colours in the brand kit and upload your fonts from dafont.com or 10001fonts.com

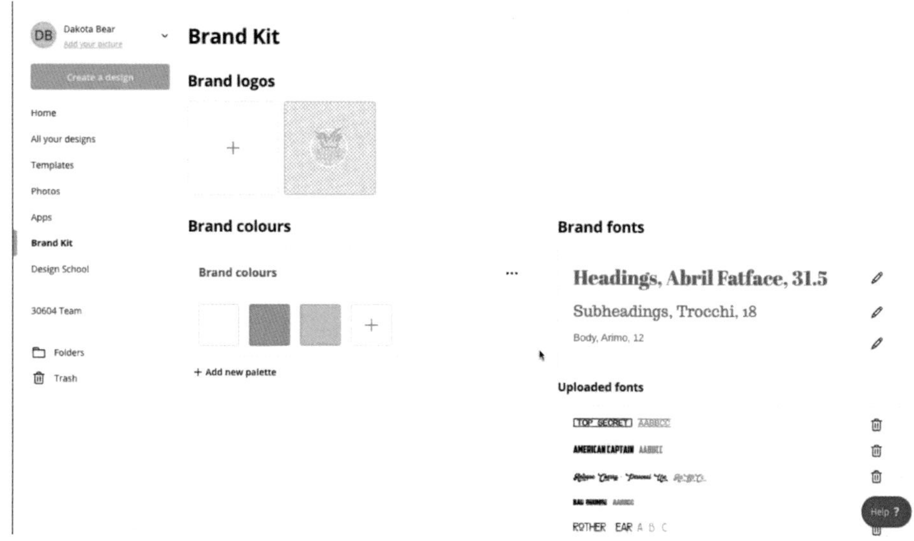

3. **Set your design up for success.** Optimize resolution at 3000 pixels by 3000 pixels. This prevents distortion.

4. **Customize.** Add your brand name and customize it with your fonts and brand colours.

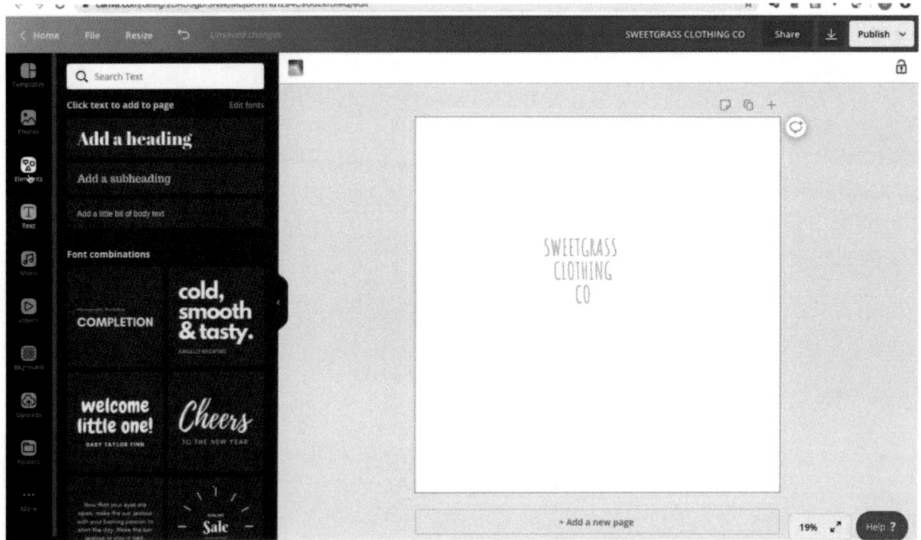

5. **Get visual.** Add in your design elements.

Download your logo with a transparent background. This makes it easy to use for a variety of projects.

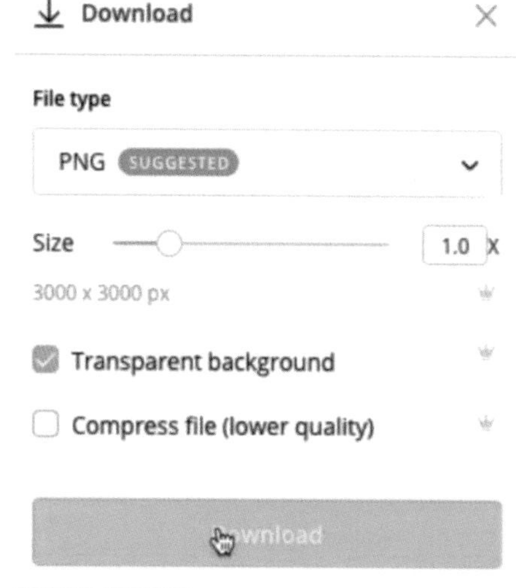

LESSON 4: PREPPING YOUR PRODUCT

"Finding the perfect product for your business is important."

Your business starts with an idea and eventually it ends up in the hands of consumers. These are Casey's tips on getting your product to market from her perspective as a clothing store owner:

Start off small. Test the waters and see how it goes.

Find your product. If you're launching a clothing line she recommends Blankapparel.ca for affordable, amazing products but says there are a lot of options out there.

Finding a tshirt printer. They put your designs on your clothing products. Phone around to find the best priced service that meets your needs and keeps your overhead low.

LESSON 5: MARKETING

"You're always working towards engaging your audience and building that online relationship with your customers. This will help to grow your online business while keeping the attention of your current customers."

If you want to sell your product or service, you need to get it in front of people. In this lesson, Casey walks us through ways to market your product or service.

SOCIAL MEDIA MARKETING

Create a Facebook page and Instagram for your brand and fill it with relevant content that brings and adds value to your business. For Sweetgrass Clothing Co, she shares about traditional medicines and traditional knowledge systems.

EMAIL MARKETING

Collect emails through your website so that you can send promotions and deals to your customers. You can retarget those customers to let them know about new offers. These same emails will help with your Facebook ads.

INFLUENCER MARKETING

Share your product with influential people who align with your brand. Ask them to post about your product and tag you to drive traffic to your website and offers.

Casey explained the difference between two concepts that sound the same but are actually different.

Advertisement: When you spend money to drive attention to your business promotions, like a commercial.

Promotions: Actions that help to spread the word on your business (like a discount or a content)

LESSON 6: WEBSITE BUILDING

In this lesson, Casey & Dakota walk us through creating a website through Wix. You'll need an email address and you can sign up for free initially. The ADI build option lets Wix do all the hard work for you coding the site so you don't have to become a coder to start your online business journey.

Here's how to get started.

1. **Pick your site type.** In the lesson, Dakota picked "Online Clothing Store".

2. **Select the functions you want.** Dakota chose instagram feed, subscribe form and chat.

3. **Customize your store.** Add the name, your profile image, brand palette and the template you want for your site.

4. **Populate your website.** Include information about you, your brand, your products or services.

5. **Check mobile preview.** Have a look at how your website is going to look in mobile view because most people will be looking at it on their phones.

6. **Add your products.** Delete the products that are pre-populated and create your

own. Click "new product", specify if it's digital or physical, add photos (Dakota's example was created in Printify), set a price and identify if it's a sale price, and include a product description.

7. **Set your product options.** Include the colours and sizes your product comes in. The "manage pricing" section helps you track your inventory.

8. **Get ready to ship.** Modify the shipping prices and policies in the Settings section.

9. **Help people buy.** Set up payment methods so customers can buy your products.

10. **Set your address.** Add your domain through Wix.

11. **Pick a hosting plan.** This will remove the ads on your site.

Once you've got orders coming in, the Store Orders section will help you track incoming funds and shipments you have to fulfill. When your shop is set up, you're ready to make sales and build your brand!

LESSON 7: FACEBOOK AND INSTAGRAM ADVERTISING

"It's not an easy thing to do, but it's a very effective tool in marketing and promoting your product."

Facebook and Instagram ads can be great ways to get in front of your audience. In this lesson, Casey and Dakota show us how it's done.

Get yourself to the right place. Type business.facebook.com into your search bar.

Set yourself up for success. Create your Facebook ad account.

Define your campaign goal. When you create your first ad, select the objective of your campaign. This helps Facebook know what to measure and how your ad should run.

Create your audience. Define the age, gender, location and interests of the people you want to have looking at your ad.

Create your campaign. Decide where you want your ads to appear, how much money you want to spend and how long you want it to run.

Create your content. You can use an existing post and amplify that or you can upload new content for your ad.

LESSON 8: WARRIOR ENTREPRENEURSHIP

"For me being a warrior entrepreneur, it means integrating my cultural values into my business model. It means not just making a product, selling a product and profiting off a product. It means that there is value put into that product. There is love and happiness sewn into the product that we're creating."

In this lesson, Casey talks about entrepreneurship through an Indigenous lens and how your identity shapes how you do business.

Casey's Tips for Warrior Entrepreneurship

Collaborate. Partner up with small businesses and other entrepreneurs out there.

Be sustainable. That looks like only using what you need, ethically sourcing your products, and knowing where your products come from.

Give back. Help your community to make it a better place, build community wherever you go and offer your knowledge and skills back to the community.

TECHNOLOGY & MENTORSHIP WITH JARED KOZAK

Jared Kozak is a Métis entrepreneur from La Rivière in Southwest Manitoba. He is the co-founder and IT (internet technology) director of DueNorth Systems in Winnipeg.

Though at one point his goal had been to work as a zookeeper, Jared has been interested in technology and software development since he was young. However, there was no internet access in the small community in which he grew up. "I had to go to my mom's house to get internet access because she lived outside of the community....but once I moved to Winnipeg, it really opened up a lot of doors for me."

In high school, Jared's IT interest and entrepreneurial spirit brought him his first professional success. Jared recognized a problem with the way tutors at his school were being coordinated, and he thought he might be able to improve the system by automating it. "I took it upon myself to submit a proposal to the principal of the school. The principal said, 'Yeah, this is great, and we want to pay you to do it,' and I was like, 'Oh man, now I've really got to step up and do it!'"

Jared spent three months developing the server and learning from the ground up. "I started Googling around, 'How do I do this thing? What is PHP? What is a web framework? How do I build this in a secure way?' And from that I made a lot of mistakes, and I learned from those mistakes."

Jared did not take this task on for the money, but simply because he enjoyed the challenge. However, he was very excited to be paid a contractor stipend from the school. "As a high school student, getting $2,000 as an influx into your bank account, that's a huge win!" It was rewarding for Jared to be paid for his product, as well as to have people appreciate and use what he made. "It was beyond belief to have something I made be used on that scale and have people talking about it; it's so cool! Unimaginable, really."

With that early encouragement, Jared continued to self-teach and to seek out mentors to advise and direct him. "For the most part, my IT-related skills have all been learned online or though mentors within my own network."

Jared went on to university, where he joined the University of Manitoba Indigenous Commerce Students, and it was only then that he began to explore his Indigenous heritage and culture. "I didn't really grow up with my Métis ancestry in mind. [At university] I started discovering who I was as an indigenous person, and where my culture and where my values came from in terms of what my ancestry was."

Jared chose to focus on business in his post-secondary education. "My biggest weakness was just the soft skills, so the skills like critical thinking, people skills, talking to people, negotiating, those kind of core skills that are fundamental to the way that business works."

For Jared, those were the critical skills he was missing. He knew he already had access to the IT information he needed through the internet, books, and of course, his mentors. Whether providing creative or technical inspiration, or just encouragement and support, Jared's mentors have had an enormous impact on his success. Mentors such as his business partner, James Warren. "I don't run my business alone. I run it with [James]. He's about 10 years older than me, and he's.... one of the most creative people that I've ever met in my life. I draw huge inspiration from him and his dedication to our business."

Another important mentor for Jared has been his mother. "My mom's an ICU nurse at the Health Sciences Centre, so she's right at the front lines of [Covid19]. She's super inspirational." Jared never takes the support of his mentors for granted: "All of my mentors are just all great, great people, and I couldn't ask for better mentors. I think I'm very lucky in my life that I've had such good mentorship."

So, it isn't surprising that Jared is offering himself as a mentor for anyone interested in the IT industry ("Just reach out on kozan.dev"). And, he recommends young people seek mentors out in the areas that interest them: "Think about someone that's in a field that you like and ask them. It never hurts to ask people to be your mentor."

CREATING DIGITAL MEDIA ON A BUDGET

Diana Hellson

View the videos in this series online! Scan the QR code, or visit http://www.tigurl.org/dmbudget

Diana Hellson, also known as MAMARUDE-GYAL MTHC and founder of Afro-Indigenous hiphop and entertainment group Rudegang Entertainment, spent years working on DIY projects and free software and wants to share how you can create digital media on a tight budget. She is a multi-disciplinary artist with a focus on hip hop, R & B, filmmaking, photography and graphic arts. Her lesson series is going to focus on her three favorite forms of digital media, which are photography, filmmaking, and graphic art.

LESSON 1: WHAT IS DIGITAL MEDIA AND WHAT CAN IT DO?

"Whether you're trying to promote your work or take over the world, having some working knowledge of digital media is definitely going to come in handy."

Some of the earliest known media in history are the last cave paintings and print media. Digital media has had such a broad and complex impact on society and culture and has caused innovative disruption in many fields of communication.

MEDIA:

the communication outlets or tools used to store and deliver data or information

These are some examples of digital media:

- instructional and educational videos and apps
- advertisements
- Music videos
- public service announcements
- video games

These are some ways people have used media to reach their goals:

- Historical preservation
- Getting elected to public office
- Event promotion

Keep following along for great tips on how to reach your goals with digital media. It doesn't have to be expensive and you don't have to be an expert to do it!

LESSON 2: GRAPHIC ART AND DESIGN

"Graphic art is what you get when art meets visual communication and communication design."

In this lesson, Diana Hellson talks about how she utilized free software to create works for herself and a variety of other artists. Graphic art has so many applications, from street signs to promotional content or deeply symbolic art pieces. It can also look like album cover art or poster art, logos, branding, or illustrations.

"Graphic art is one of my favorite forms of digital media, because it gives me all the freedom to explore shape and scale and color in ways that are not typically available to me in real life."

Diana talks about how most artists and companies will agree that having the prettiest or the dopest or the cleanest or the butteriest branding and marketing is an essential goal that should always be in your game plan.

You don't need a lot of things to get started. Just software and maybe a tablet. Diana uses her tablet that connects to her laptop so she can draw her illustration directly into the software of her choosing.

Tablets can range in price from very affordable to very pricey, but they're a great addition to your arsenal. That said, you don't actually need one to create great graphic art. You can still do node based editing. Diana sometimes moves the nodes individually, perfectly into place until her outlines are crisp.

Here are some examples of free software that can be helpful:

- Vector
- SVG Edit
- Inkscape

These are some software examples that offer free subscriptions:

- Photoshop
- Adobe
- InDesign
- Adobe illustrator

These are some mobile apps you can use on your phone:

- Canva
- Create
- Photoshop Express
- Tayasui Sketches

"Feeling lost and making mistakes is all part of the process. When you're developing a new skill, don't let it discourage you."

You can learn how to use software through Youtube tutorials, online research and connecting with other members of the arts community. Reach out and connect to resources and community to make your graphic art dreams happen!

LESSON 3: PHOTOGRAPHY

"Photographs are among the most powerful forms of digital media because of the way they capture an exact moment in the blink of an eye."

Once inaccessible and expensive, photography has become more accessible through advancements in technology. Photo editing has also become low cost and user friendly. Cameras themselves are no longer heavy and we don't have to rely on dark rooms to process our work.

You don't need an expensive DSLR camera to make great photographs. These days cell phones are equipped with some of the finest tiny cameras on the market. If you have a smartphone, you're good to go.

These are some free photo editing software choices to help you transform the photos you take on your phone:

- Photoshop Express
- Canva
- Photoscape
- Photoshop's free trial

You don't need a computer to edit your photos either, you can do it all on your phone with these apps:

- Adobe Lightroom
- VSCO
- Snapseed
- Pixart

You can learn how to use all of this software through YouTube tutorials. Now, get out there and start taking photos!

LESSON 4: FILM

"Film allows us to communicate our thoughts, feelings, messages, current events, and works of art out to the masses."

In this lesson, Diana explains how she used free film editing software to create some of the very first Rudegang videos. Just like photography, videography has become more accessible with the arrival of the smartphone. No longer exclusive to Hollywood insiders, making videos is something that can be done easily by everyday people.

Here are some things you can do with film:

- Create meaningful content that has a positive impact
- Connect with clients, friends, family, and supporters
- Event promotion
- Music Sharing
- Share about upcoming opportunities

"Whatever your communication goals may be, film and video creation are certain to be your most reliable and effective means of reaching your audience."

You don't need a big, expensive video camera or DSLR, your smartphone can work just fine, too. If you do need something high tech, look into local camera rental so you don't have to buy all the equipment yourself. GoPro led panels or a DSLR can be rented weekly at a relatively low cost.

Once you have shot your video, you can edit it in free software like:

- Blender
- Shotcut
- Imovie
- Davinci Resolve

These free options can help you edit, colorize and soundmaster. Paid options like Final Cut Pro 10, Premier Pro or any other high end video editing software offer much higher quality definition, color, and rendering. Once again, don't forget to take advantage of YouTube tutorials to learn how to use all this great software.

Now that you know the basics of what digital media is, what you can do with graphic art, photography and film, you're ready to make low cost art all by yourself. There are so many ways to learn these digital skills online through free tutorials so not having a budget doesn't have to hold you back from making digital magic.

ACTORS KIT

Jimmy Blais

View the videos in this series online! Scan the QR code, or visit http://www.tigurl.org/actorskit

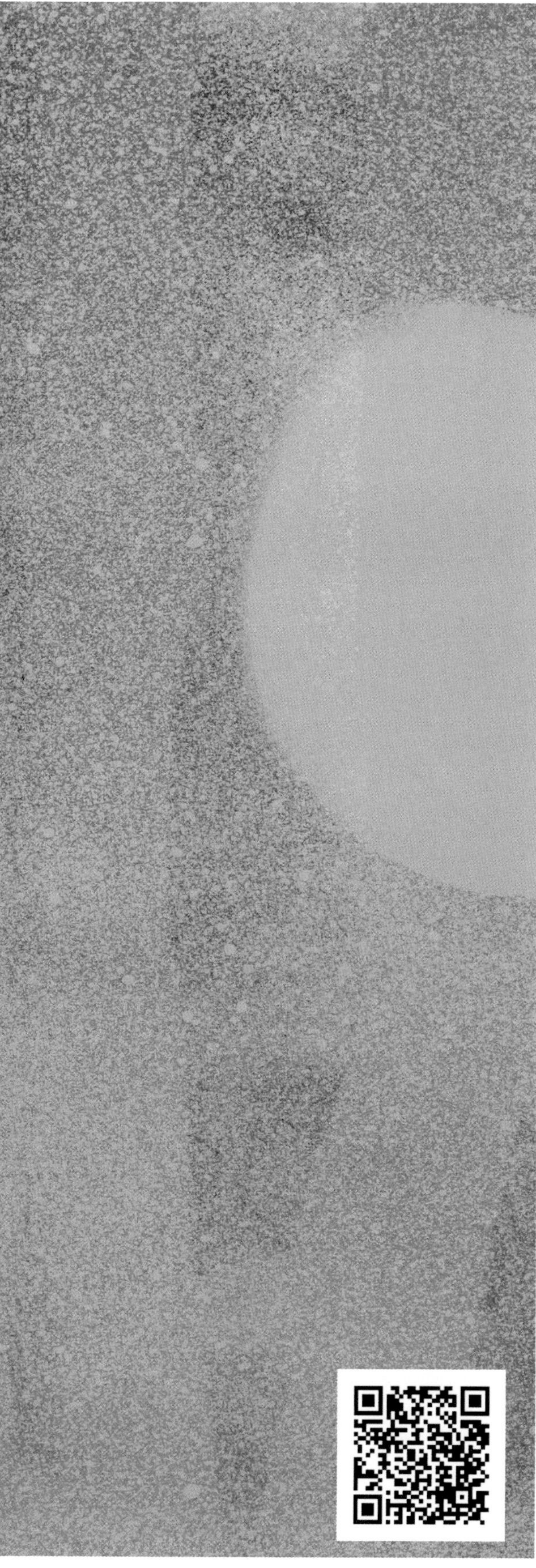

Actor Jimmy Blais brought us this 4 part series on the essentials of what you will need as an emerging actor. Tune in and learn how to make your mark as an actor and get started today. These lessons will include how to prepare for an audition, how to create a self-tape at home for an audition, how to create a video demo reel and how to create an audio demo reel. These are the key components you need to address if you want to get an agent or promote yourself in order to get an audition for a part with producers or directors.

LESSON 1: AUDITION PREP

If you want to nail your audition, there are a few key things you are going to want to do.

READ EVERYTHING:
That includes:

1. The body of the email that you get with your audition requests. Pay attention to the audition date, audition time, location, and information about the character.

2. The sides. That's the script you're going to be using for the audition.

3. The Breakdown. That's the breakdown of your character: age, race, job, relationship details, as well as character traits. It will also include the name of the project and the name of the director.

BE A DETECTIVE:
Do your research. You really need to be a detective.

1. Use the info provided to connect the dots on what the casting director or producer are looking for

2. Check out the director's previous work, watch previous episodes or parts and try to get a feel for the project. It will help you understand what kind of mood or feeling the producers are gone for and the genre.

READ THE SCRIPT... AGAIN AND AGAIN:
Read the script as many times as you can. This will help you learn:

1. Your lines.

2. Your cues.

3. Stage directions.

You will get a better sense of the action of the scene if you read the script thoroughly. Read dialogue that isn't part of your scene if you have access to it. Read the full script if it's publicly available so you have a big picture sense of the story and an ability to portray your character more sharply. You may get less information in movie or tv auditions but use what you get to your advantage.

BE PREPARED.
Get ready for your audition and make sure to:

1. Practice the script out loud. It's different than practicing in your head.

2. Get a reader. Find a friend who will read the other character's lines in the scene to help you practice.

3. Dress the part. Read the breakdown and dress accordingly. Alternately, dress as neutrally as possible, try not to wear any bright colors or any big logos. Keep the focus on your performance and off of what you're wearing.

4. Put your best foot forward. Try not to wear noisy shoes that too will draw attention away from your performance.

HAVE FUN.
The more prepared you are, the more fun you will have. The director might have different ideas when you arrive so if you're prepared and loose, you can roll with changes in direction with more grace.

Now, get ready to nail your audition! Break a leg!

LESSON 2: HOW TO DO A SELF-TAPE

You might not always be able to audition in person. A self-tape lets you record your audition for if you are in a different city or unavailable to attend in person. You can use a company to produce your self-tape or you can do it at home.

Here's how to make the most of your self-tape:

FIND A WALL.
A plain wall with nothing hanging on it works best. You might think making the background more interesting would be better but that's not the case. Too much clutter, like, this, can be distracting:

This is a better option, because it keeps the focus on you and your performance.

SET UP YOUR EQUIPMENT.

Your phone on a tripod with a light will work great. Jimmy got his set up on Amazon for under $70. If you don't have a tripod or light setup, you can improvise with what you have around the house. Set yourself up near a window or use lamps in front of you and behind your camera, not behind you. Set the camera at eye level or just above eye level and make sure you're filming in landscape, not portrait. Filming from below creates a double chin.

NEXT PIECE TO CONSIDER IS YOUR EYE LINE.
When you're performing with your reader or your scene partner, you're going to want to do some tests in terms of where you're looking.

EYELINE:

where you're looking when you're acting

When your eye line is like this, looking at your partner, you can't really see your eyes.

On the other hand, you don't want to get too close to the camera so you're staring right at it.

Your final product should look something like this:

Now you're ready to record your self-tape. Lights, camera, action!

LESSON 3: HOW TO CREATE A DEMO REEL

DEMO REEL: a compilation of scenes you put on video to demonstrate yourself as an actor

Your demo reel helps you show off your skills to talent agents, producers or casting houses. You can create a great demo reel even if you don't have existing footage of yourself. At that point, you're going to be making a self-tape.

Here's how to create your demo reel:

TRY TO AVOID USING ONLY COMEDIC SCENES OR ONLY DRAMATIC SCENES. MIX IT UP!
Find yourself a couple of good contrasting scenes online. The contrast will show your range as an actor. Avoid scenes with the same tone or that promote you in the same way as an actor. Show all your sides so people know how versatile you can be.

THIS GOES FOR TYPES OF CHRACTER AS WELL
Go to websites that offer free scripts to find scenes for your demo reel. Ask actor friends which scenes they think you would be great in.

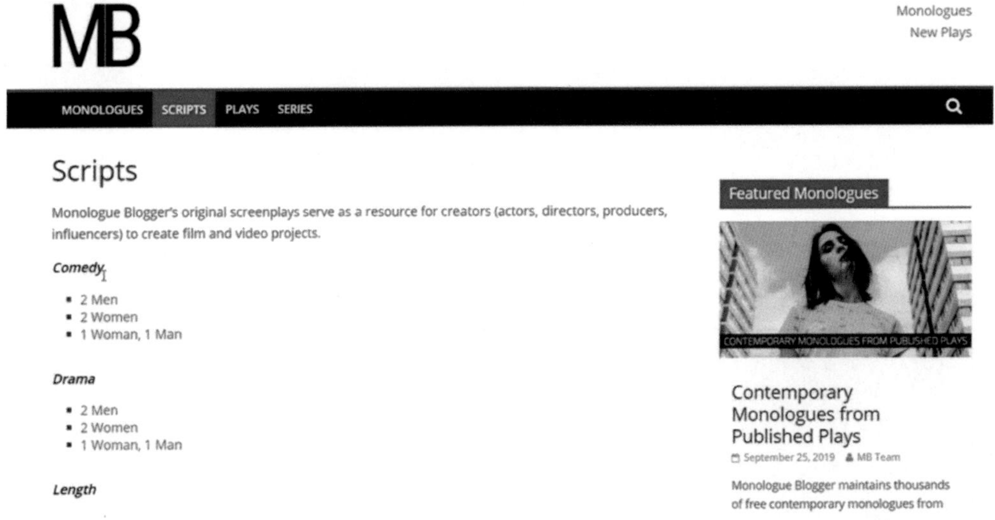

PARTNER UP
Get yourself a reader and practice until it's camera ready. Repeat the process for your next scene.

GET READY TO CONNECT.
Include your contact information at the beginning or end so people can hire you.

KEEP IT SIMPLE.

Don't get fancy with your editing, a quick, clean transition is all you need. You can use iMovie on your Mac, pre-loaded video editing software on your PC or you can upgrade to Adobe Premiere (which often has a free 7 day trial.) You can hire a demo reel editing service if you can afford to, it's a great option if you have existing footage or if you are new to editing. Also, keep your reel to between 3 and 5 minutes.

CHECK OUT THE COMPETITION

Have a look at other actor's demo reels on talent agent's websites to get a feel for what they are like before you solidify your final product.

A good demo reel will help you get an agent and an agent will help you get hired. Now you have the information you need to get started. Good luck and have fun!

LESSON 4: HOW TO CREATE A VOICE DEMO REEL

Like a regular demo reel, a voice demo reel is meant to swell you as an actor. The voice demo reel sets you up to land projects like these (and you should have a different one for each category). Within those categories, you can have different voices and characters you work into them:

- Animation
- Video game
- Commercial
- Narration

You can record a voice demo reel at home but you might need to upgrade your equipment. A condenser mic, a filter and a pre-amp can go a long way and don't have to be expensive. Even a usb microphone you can plug into your computer is an upgrade over your phone microphone. The audio editing software Audacity is free online and there are lots of YouTube tutorials available online to learn how to use it.

You're going to want to use music to set the mood for your voice work. You can find royalty-free music online on sites like freeplaymusic.com where you can search by style:

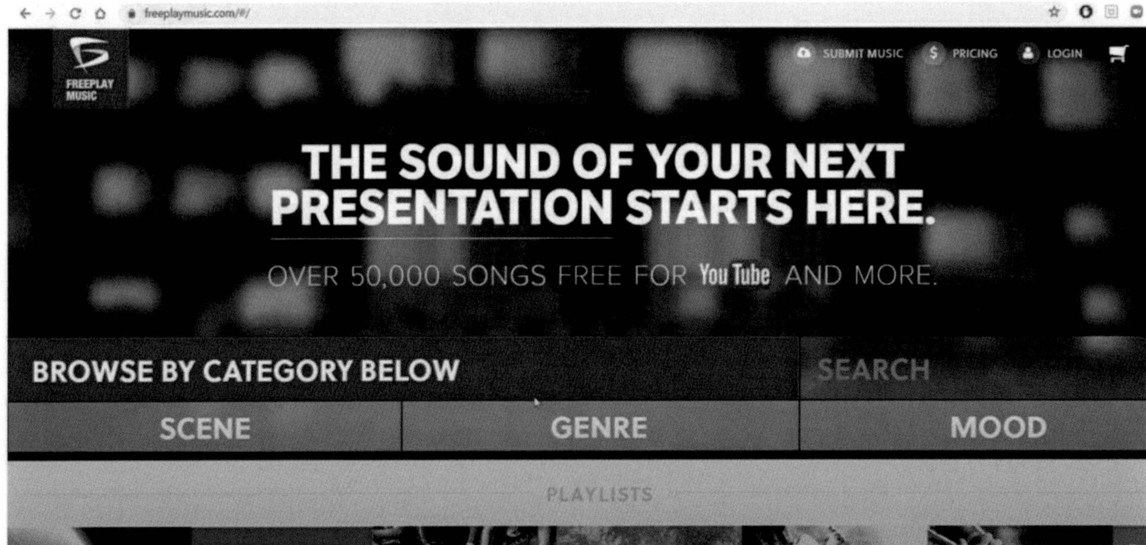

CHECK OUT THE COMPETITION

Just like your demo reel, have a listen to other voice actor's voice demo reels to get a feel for them.

Voice demo reels are shorter than video demo reels and should run 1.5-2 minutes. Typically casting people can tell right away if they will pick you so lead with your best work.

SCRIPT YOURSELF FOR SUCCESS

You can find voice actor scripts for a variety of assignment types online on websites like voices.com

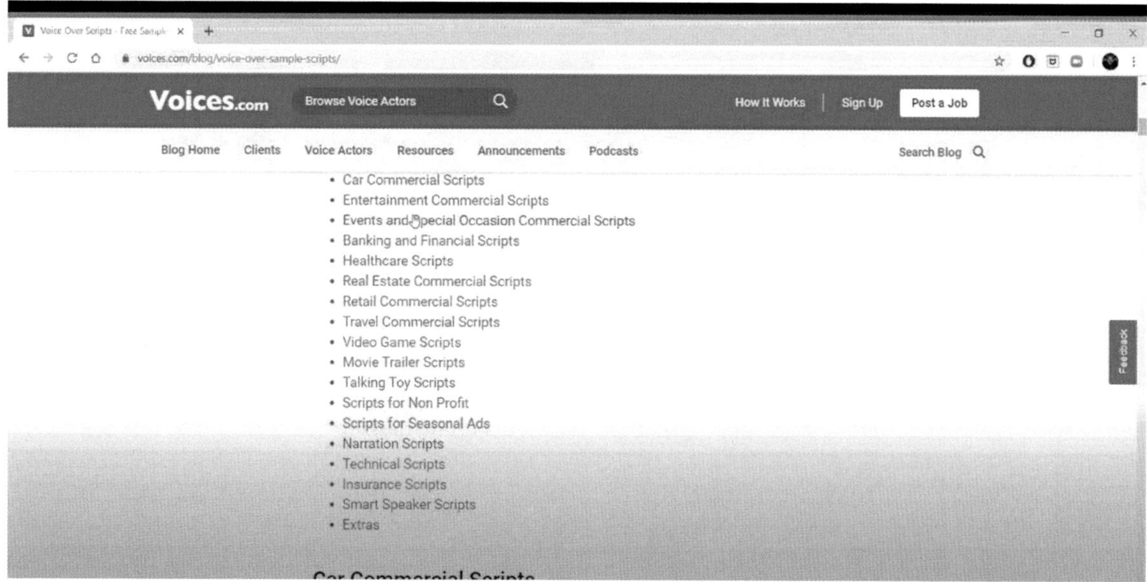

PRACTICE MAKES PERFECT

Practice the scripts you're going to use over and over again so you're ready when it's time to record.

GET YOURSELF SITUATED

If you're recording somewhere that isn't a professional booth, get into a small room, like a closet full of clothes. You can also cover yourself and your microphone with a blanket to contain the sound and dampen background noise.

Once you have headshots, a demo reel, and a voice demo reel, you're ready to start shopping yourself around to agents. As you book work, integrate those projects into your demo reels.

And.... scene! Now you've got what you need to know to start your career as an actor. Get out there and make magic!

FILM YOURSELF LIKE A BOSS

Patrick Shannon

View the videos in this series online! Scan the QR code, or visit http://www.tigurl.org/filmboss

Patrick Shannon, also known as Nang K̲'uulas, is an Indigenous-Canadian film-maker, social entrepreneur and activist from the remote island nation of Haida Gwaii, off the Northwest coast of Canada.

Patrick's award-winning work centres around social and cultural justice, and the elevation of marginalized voices through education, youth mentorship, media, and technology.

LESSON 1: INTERVIEWING YOURSELF

YOUR NARRATIVE

In this series, you will learn how to create a short film that introduces yourself and your stories to the world. This is a great way to self-promote, especially as artists, creators or public figures. This tutorial uses cell phone video footage because it doesn't matter what equipment you use, it matters how you use it.

WICKED INTERVIEW

Here's what you need to think about when you're going to interview yourself for your video:

The right tools.

Use the voice memo app to record your voice.

The right place.

Find somewhere quiet, avoiding noisy appliances like heating units and refrigerators. Closets are a great choice because they absorb sound and help you avoid the "empty" sound.

Use your equipment the right way.

Hold the microphone 12 inches from your face. Any closer, you will risk plosives.

Don't stress about mistakes. You can always take the best takes and edit things later.

PLOSIVES:

bursts of air that hit the microphone when you pronounce P's or B's.

Drink Up!

Hydration is key to avoiding icky, sticky noises. When you haven't had enough water, your saliva gets sticky. Chugging water, right before recording isn't any better because it just gives you a moist mouth. Drink lots of water about one to two hours before recording to stop your mouth from getting sticky or too moist.

Add energy

Don't let yourself sound monotone, let your voice get higher and lower. You don't want to sound boring.

Now for the part people worry about the most... what do you say?

Questions to ask yourself:

- Who are you?
- How'd you get started?
- What inspires you?
- What is your favorite part of doing what you do?

- What are things that you've learned?
- What are your hopes for the future?
- And finally, any parting thoughts for the people?

Now you're set to record your video and to film yourself like a boss.

LESSON 2: SHOOTING YOUR FOOTAGE

With our wicked interview ready to go, we just need some slick looking footage. Since we won't be speaking directly on camera, we need B-roll.

If you were filming someone in an interview, that would be your main shot. B roll could be closeups of your subjects hands, or footage of them outside, drawing, or filming.

B ROLL:

footage that is supplemental to your main shot.

Here's how to pick what to shoot:
Listen through your interview and pick out things that you could film.

Create a shotlist. That's a point form list of shots that you want to get to put over top of your interview. Other examples are shots of you doing your work or doing things that you enjoy. Get shots of objects that you work around your tools, your space, things that bring you joy and show your personality.

- Some trees
- Closeup of my hands
- wide shots of the cultural centre
- close ups of the poles and canoe
- my goofy face

Go out and get your footage.

FILMING TIPS:

- Always make sure to shoot in landscape orientation, unless you're intentionally delivering to mobile platforms like TikTok.
- Make sure your footage is properly exposed. Don't let it get too light or too dark.
- Slow it Down.

Shoot some Slow Mo.
Set your camera to film at a higher frame rate, like 60 frames a second, or even 120 frames a second. You can slow it down when you're editing to get nice and silky smooth shots.

Frame Rates:
Most movies are shot at 24 Frames per Second. News and sports is typically shot around 30 and that's often the default of your phone

PATRICK'S TIPS:

I always recommend shooting at 24 frames a second. It just looks more cinematic, but you can always shoot it, whatever you want. It's all personal preference.

I also recommend shooting in 1080P resolution. That's typically the best mixture of quality and file size for video. You can shoot at 4k, but that'll take up way more space and isn't really necessary.

If you're filming yourself, use a tripod. If you're not using a tripod, make sure you keep your footage super steady. Nothing looks more amateur like shaky handheld footage.

HOW TO GET SHOTS THAT WILL MAKE YOUR VIDEO MORE EXCITING:
Lock your elbows and do some slow sweeping movements. Think of it like Tai Chi, but with the camera.

Get high

Get low.

Pan side to side.

Get close.

Go wide.

Get lots. It's always better to grab more than you initially think you need.

Try to hold a shot for at least five to 10 seconds. That just gives you more to work with later.

Now you've interviewed yourself, got the footage you need to make your video and you've filmed yourself like a boss!

MUSIC MAKERS 101

Dakota Bear

View the videos in this series online! Scan the QR code, or visit http://www.tigurl.org/music101

"I want to pass along the skills and knowledge, the tools and resources that I've learned throughout this 10 years to help you and your music career as an artist."

Dakota started his music journey at 16, recording his own songs and videos, and throwing his own shows. He's recorded over 350 songs and has about a hundred videos out online with a million views.

Dakota has been on twice, with his third tour postponed due to COVID. He's been featured in magazines, newspapers, and radio. He's won best Aboriginal video and best hip hop video from the Canadian Independent Music Video Awards.

Dakota got his music business knowhow through Nimbus, an 8-month program that taught him music business management, how to navigate through the music industry and then apply that knowledge with his partner to launch their clothing line.

In this series, Dakota Bear is going to be discussing everything from songwriting, marketing, promotions, distribution, getting your song ready, how to create the artwork, all the way to publicity and promotion, all for beginners. You'll also learn something if you've been doing this for a while.

If you're building a business, these skills are very much transferable. When Dakota first started doing music, he did everything from burning the CDs, recording, putting the CDs as a package together and then hustling out of his backpack in high school. He learned from YouTube, Google, tutorials, and his schooling.

> *"Putting all of that knowledge together has really helped me in my path as a hip hop artist, as a musician entering the music industry."*

SONGWRITING

> *"When I first started out, I never even knew what a bar was. I never knew what a melody was. I had the gift of writing. I wrote short stories. I wrote poems. I didn't listen to any hip hop until I was about 14 years old and I never wrote any hip hop songs until I was about 14 years old. I got my recording equipment when I was 16. So when I was 16 years old, I still was unsure what a bar was. I didn't know how to structure the song at all."*

In this lesson, we're going to be learning about songwriting. This first part of songwriting we're going to be talking about is structure. It's very important that you know how to structure your song.

A song is usually made up of two parts. You have your verse, and then you have your chorus. Your verse is made up of 16 bars. Your chorus is made up of eight bars within the beat. Sometimes you'll have the hook first. Sometimes you'll have the verse first. You'll really have to load your beat into your software and take a look at it, take a listen and see what is coming first. In Dakota's song, Freedom, it was the verse that came first and then the hook came after that.

BAR:

A bar is a measurement in music, a grouping together of four beats.

Dakota learned music without a mentor, using what he could learn online.

> *"It was just really me and my computer and teaching myself everything that I needed to know to ensure that I was able to go on the beat, flow properly, catch the melodies. And it, of course, took a lot of time. It took a lot of practice."*

BREAKING IT DOWN

"When I was writing my songs and I learned what a bar was, I didn't even need a beat. Sometimes I was just like one, two, three, four, one, two, three, four, and there's a lot of rhythm to it. I had to learn that rhythm. I had to learn those melodies. But it's easier the more that you practice and the more that you're writing your lyrics down, when you're finding your beats, or if you don't have a beat, you can just do that count in your head."

There are four beats in one bar. You have 16 bars in your verse and within that 16 bars, you're going to have beats. Those beats will be kicks, snares, and drums. It'll be broken down 16 times for your verse and then another eight times for your hook.

"Now that you know that the song is broken up in two parts, your hooks and your verses and you know that there's beats in between each bar, it's going to help you catch those melodies. It's going to help you when you're writing your songs."

"I always wanted to rap fast. I just didn't know how this makes it much easier."

Dakota uses his MacBook that has GarageBand and often records with Rob the Viking. In GarageBand you can set the bar, the beat and the tempo. You can adjust the tempo depending on if you want a slow or fast song. If you don't have GarageBand, you can google metronome and use a web-based tool.

TEMPO:

the pace of a song, expressed in beats per minute.

METRONOME:

a tool for counting out beats which helps keep music on time.

Now that you know about the structure of songwriting, you can start making music.

LESSON 3: SONGWRITING PART 2

"Music is therapeutic. It's healing. It's a way to express ourselves."

In this lesson, Dakota Bear takes us behind the scenes of his own writing process:

"First, I find my flow. Before I start writing my bars. I'll find the flow on the beat. I'll listen to it over and over and over and over again. Don't rush through your songs. You don't have to make a song in one or two hours."

AUTHENTICITY IN SONGWRITING

"Take your time with your craft. Practice as much as you can. As indigenous peoples, we're natural storytellers. So tell your story. Where do you come from? Who are you? What do you stand for?"

Dakota talks about the importance of being true to yourself in music and how songwriting can be therapeutic and healing like journaling. When it comes to writer's block, Dakota recommends writing every day, whether you're writing songs, journaling in a book or on your phone.

As a genre, hip hop can glorify the wrong things, Dakota observes, and notes that it's important to consider the impact of your words on your audience. He also encourages songwriting as a way for Indigenous people to represent themselves in music.

BEING WHO YOU ARE IN MUSIC

"Don't be afraid of who you are, your identity. You're unique and make sure that you show that every time that you're writing a song. Speak your truth. Write about the struggles in your community. Write about the struggles that we face as Indigenous peoples. Write about the things that are sacred to spread your light, uplifting and empowering with your song. Spring all of the things that you want to see into your future onto the track. Speak it into existence. Sometimes we feel empowered. We feel confident. Sometimes we feel frustrated, angry, sad. Let all of that out on a song."

RHYMING PATTERNS

When you're talking about rhyming patterns, it's really going back to poetry but it can be confusing.

This is an example of end rhymes:

I pray to God because sometimes I feel the odds against me.
I put my soul into the songs and tell them my heart is empty.
This is my story.
And trust when I say is far from ending.
Will I make it to the top? I guess it's all depending.

Multi-syllable rhymes are more complex and can be achieved by adding language to describe the word that is your end rhyme. If you're struggling with writer's block, try making lists of words and lists of description words. Match the words up and see what works. In the video, Dakota offers an isolation rap to illustrate a multi-syllable rhyme.

With more ideas to help your songwriting, you're well on your way to being ready to record your music.

END RHYMES:

Rhymes at the end of a phrase

INTERNAL RHYMES:

Rhymes inside of the bar

LESSON 4: RECORDING

When Dakota first started doing hip hop, he had a microphone and a computer and didn't even know how to plug the microphone into the computer. He also had an interface which made it a little bit more confusing. This lesson focuses on getting started with recording and getting what you need to build your recording equipment from scratch.

WHAT DO YOU REALLY NEED?

Get: a USB microphone that plugs right into your computer.

Skip: the interface for your recording software. You don't have to worry too much about mixing and all of that just yet. You just want to get started recording.

Get: software to record your songs on. You can use Pro Tools, which is for beginners and experts. It costs $20-30 monthly but it will help you mix your own music in the long run. Free options are GarageBand and Audacity. Audacity has limited functionality but is a good starting point. Dakota uses GarageBand for his rough recordings.

Get: YouTube tutorials and tutorials you can find on Google to help you learn how to use your recording software.

Protip: You can always send your music out to someone to mix it for you, you don't have to necessarily learn how to do it yourself.

HOW TO USE GARAGEBAND

When you open up the software, it asks you to choose a track type. Click on audio and press create.

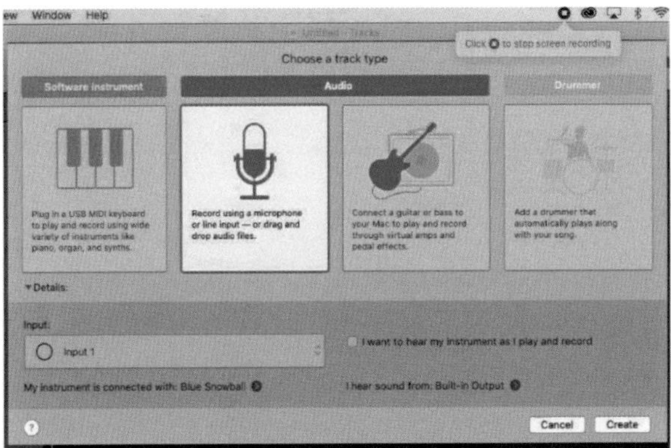

In this example we've got a beat on top and a verse down below.

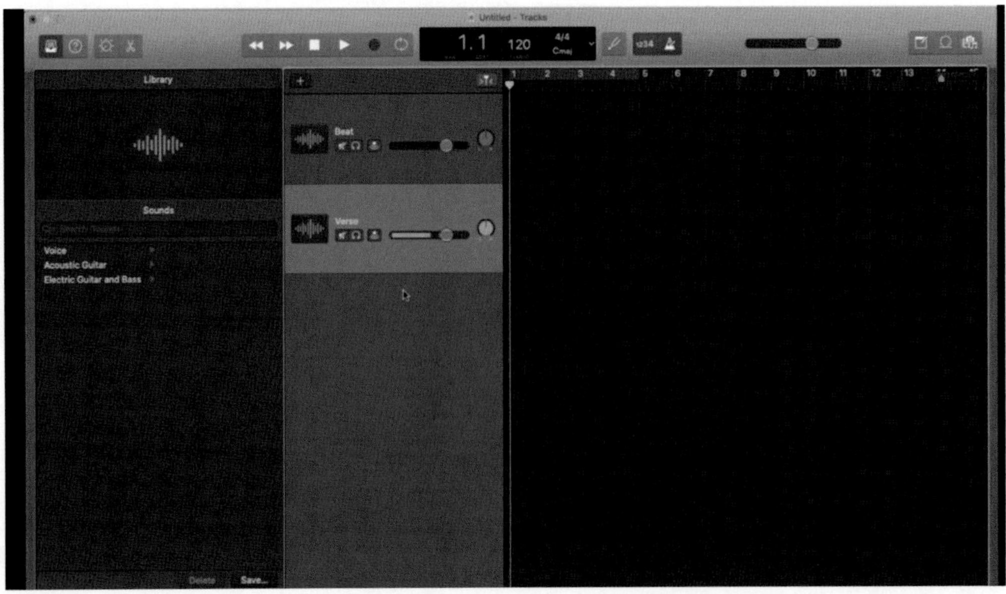

Select a file on your computer and drop it in your beat.

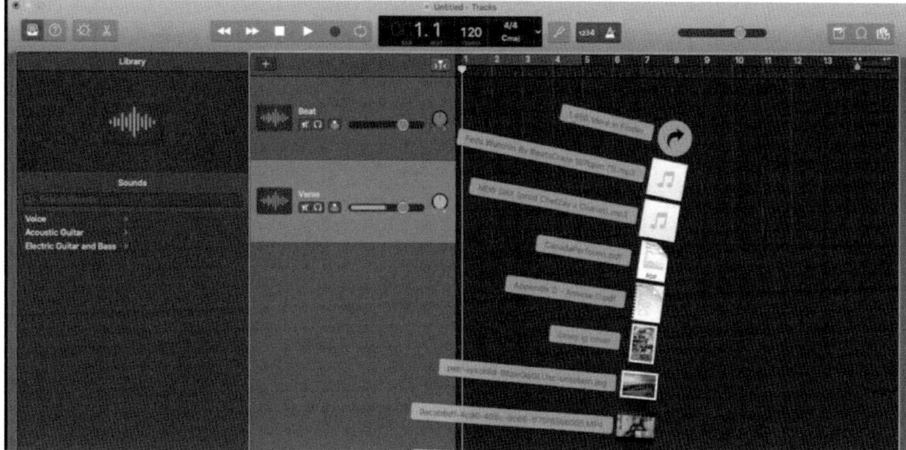

Highlight your verse. Select where on the timeline of the track that you want your verse to start and hit record.

When you record, it will look like this:

You can adjust the volume of your vocals like this and you can do the same for the beat volume on its volume adjustment function.

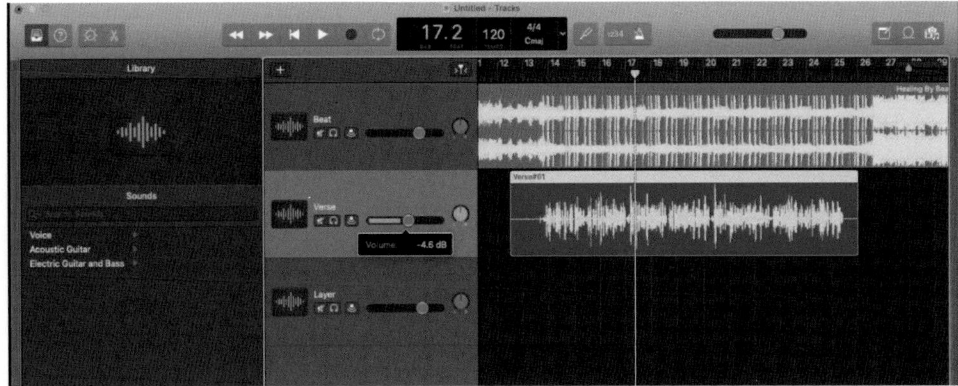

The interface layout for Garageband is similar to the layout of Pro Tools with the beat on top and the vocals underneath. You can also add effects to your track:

You can also use the onboard autotune function to make adjustments to your sound.

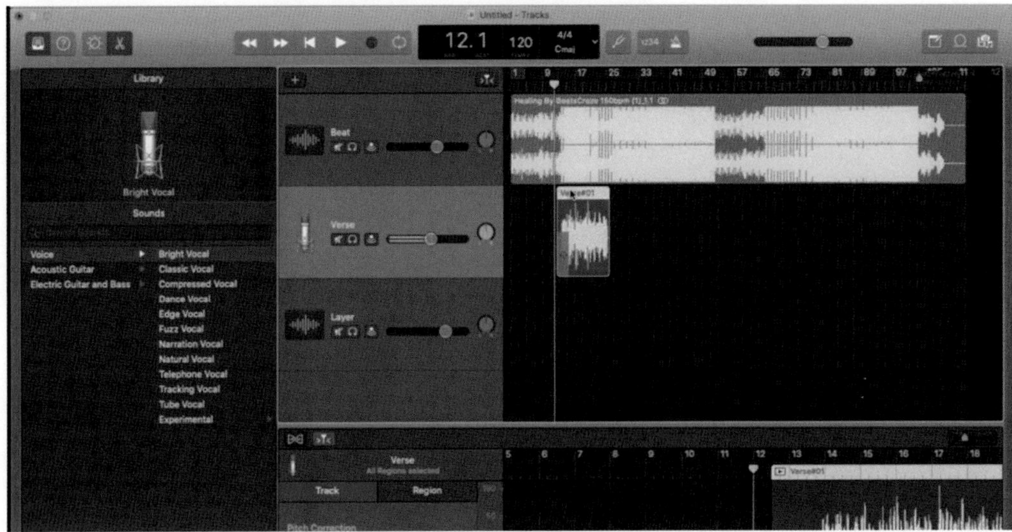

You don't need a lot to get started recording your own songs or producing your own music. Check out tutorials to learn more and make more music.

LESSON 5: ARTWORK

Artwork is important because once you have your song, you've recorded it, you've got your mix done and you want to upload it, you will need some artwork to go with it. Artwork lets your audience know what the song's going to be about and what the vibe is going to be.

Dakota likes to personalize his artwork. He combines photos, text and his logo to create custom art to get his audience excited about the music that is coming. You don't have to be a professional graphic designer to make an impression.

THE RIGHT TOOLS

Dakota uses Canva or Ribbet to create custom artwork for his music. Ribbet is free software online you can use to cut out photos, repurpose them and otherwise design some great art.

Canva is also free online, but the upgraded version lets you make art with transparent backgrounds which is very helpful, especially if you're making a logo because you don't want a white or black or gray background on your logo. It costs about $12/month to upgrade. If you're looking for a tutorial on how to use it, Casey Desjarlais' Instagram has some great lessons about that and branding.

How to Use Canva

Click 'Create a design' to get started.

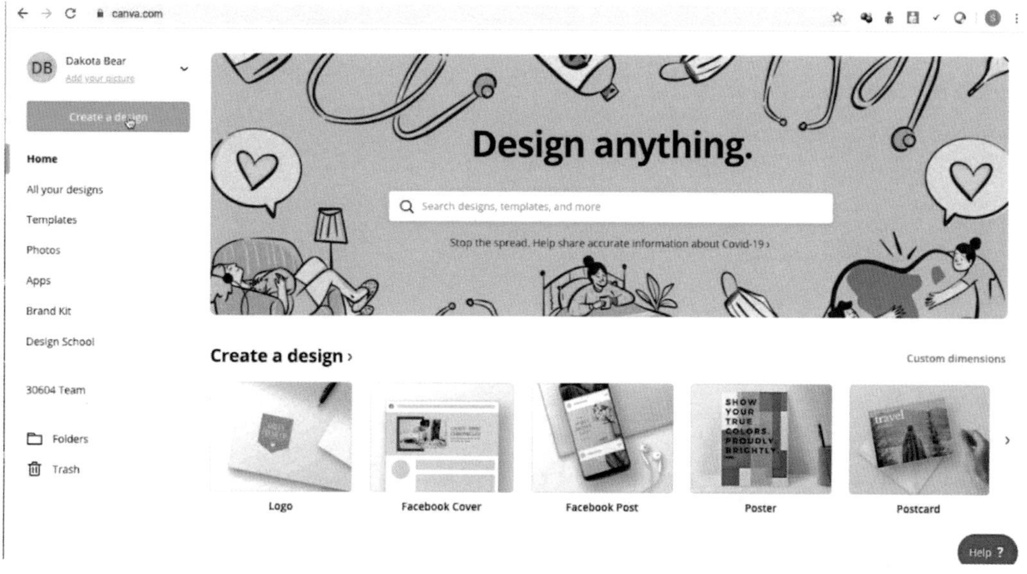

After selecting "Custom dimensions", enter the size you want your design to be. We've used 3000 x 3000.

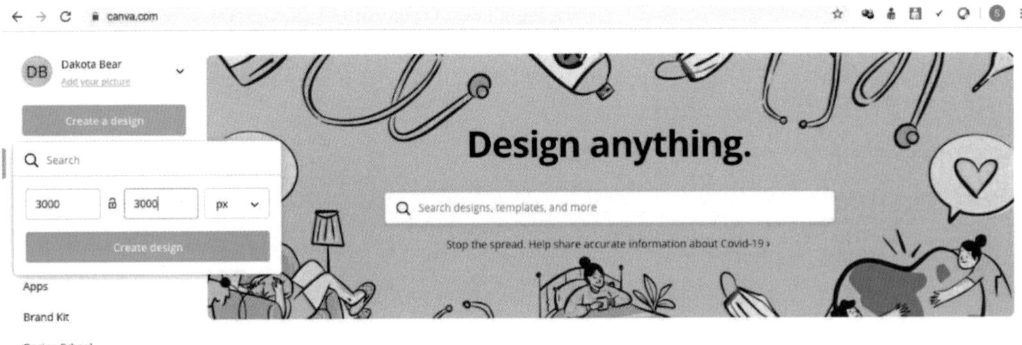

While there are templates and backgrounds available, another great resource for free photos is Unsplash.

Download the image you want, upload it to your canvas in Canva and resize the image.

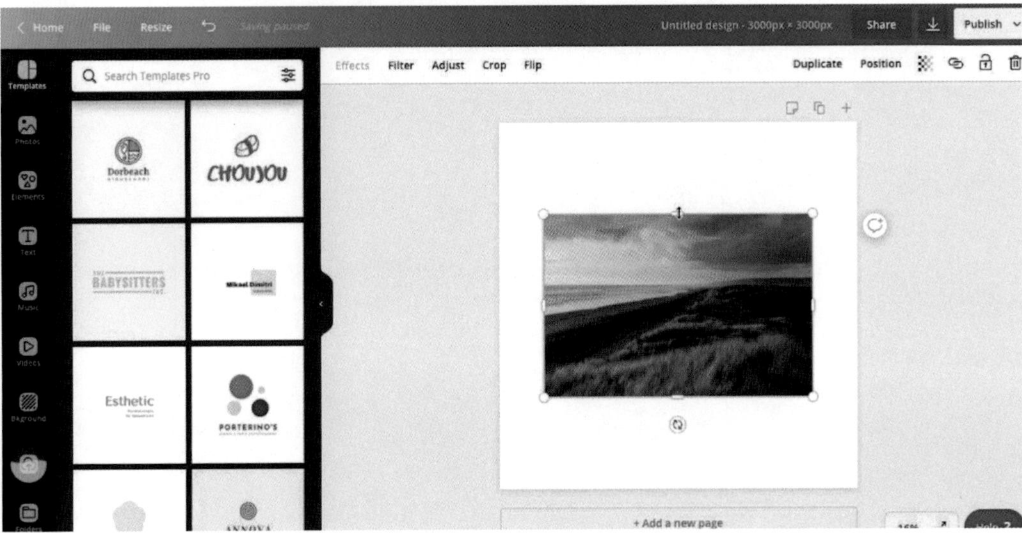

You can adjust the opacity of the image like this:

You can add filters to the images too:

You can add and customize stylized text. You can adjust the alignment and change how the text is situated, shifting it to the center or the right.

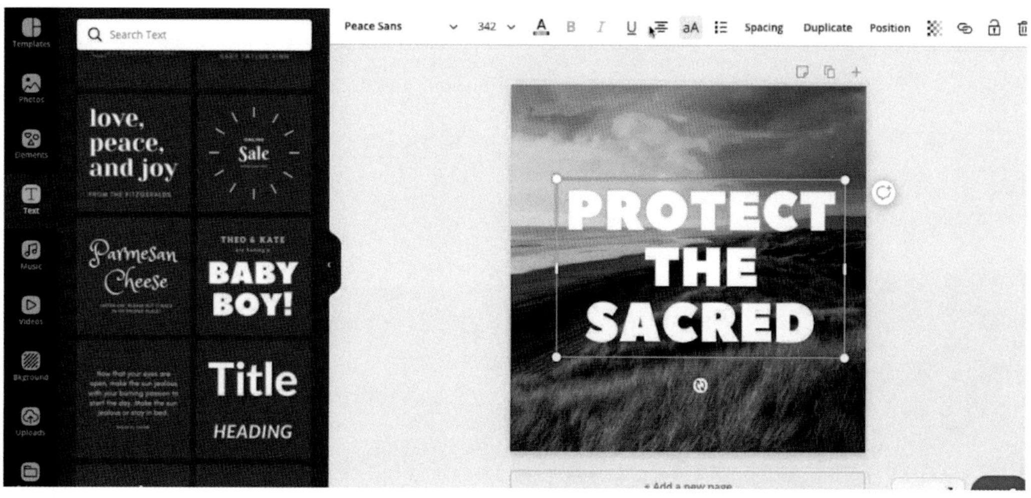

You can add your logo to the image:

Download your high-resolution image and you're good to go.

You wrote your song, you recorded it, now you've got your artwork. We're going to go onto the next phase, which is getting your music heard and distributed.

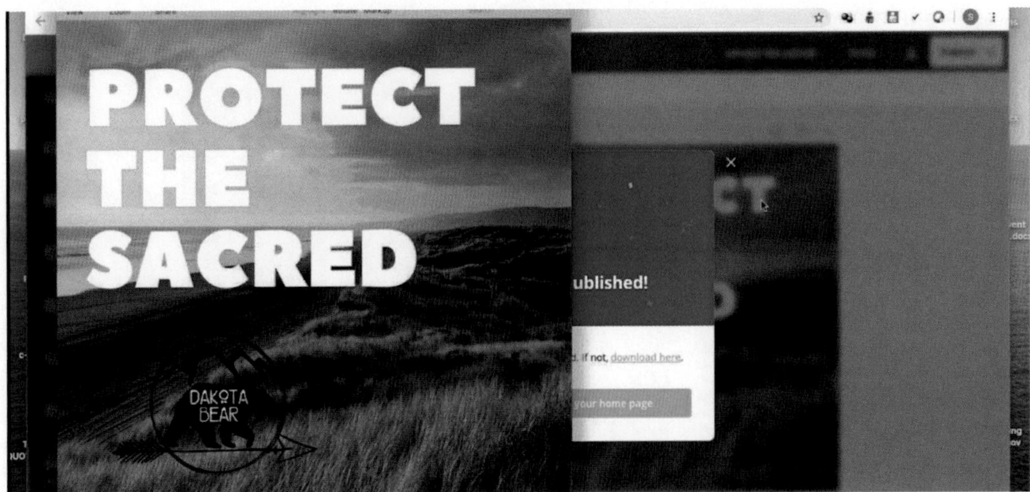

LESSON 6: DISTRIBUTION

In this lesson, we're going to be talking about distribution. You have your song and your artwork and you're ready to share your gifts with the world and start making some money off of it. You have to ensure that the instrumental that you purchased online gives you the right to sell that online with your song.

Click on the contract that you would have gotten from the producer when you bought the beat. Look at all of the things that you're allowed to do with it. Sometimes it's unlimited royalty-free (you have all the rights to it), and sometimes there are restrictions on it.

There are a number of distributors online, including TuneCore, CDBaby, and DistroKid. Dakota uses DistroKid to get his music on Apple Music, Spotify, and Title because it's the most inexpensive, paid yearly and has unlimited uploads.

HERE'S HOW YOU UPLOAD TO DISTROKID:

Select where you want your music distributed. Select the number of songs. Note if the song has been previously released. Enter your name or your band's name. Mark off if you're already in Apple Music or Spotify, set your release date, and if you want people to be able to preorder. Write in your record label name.

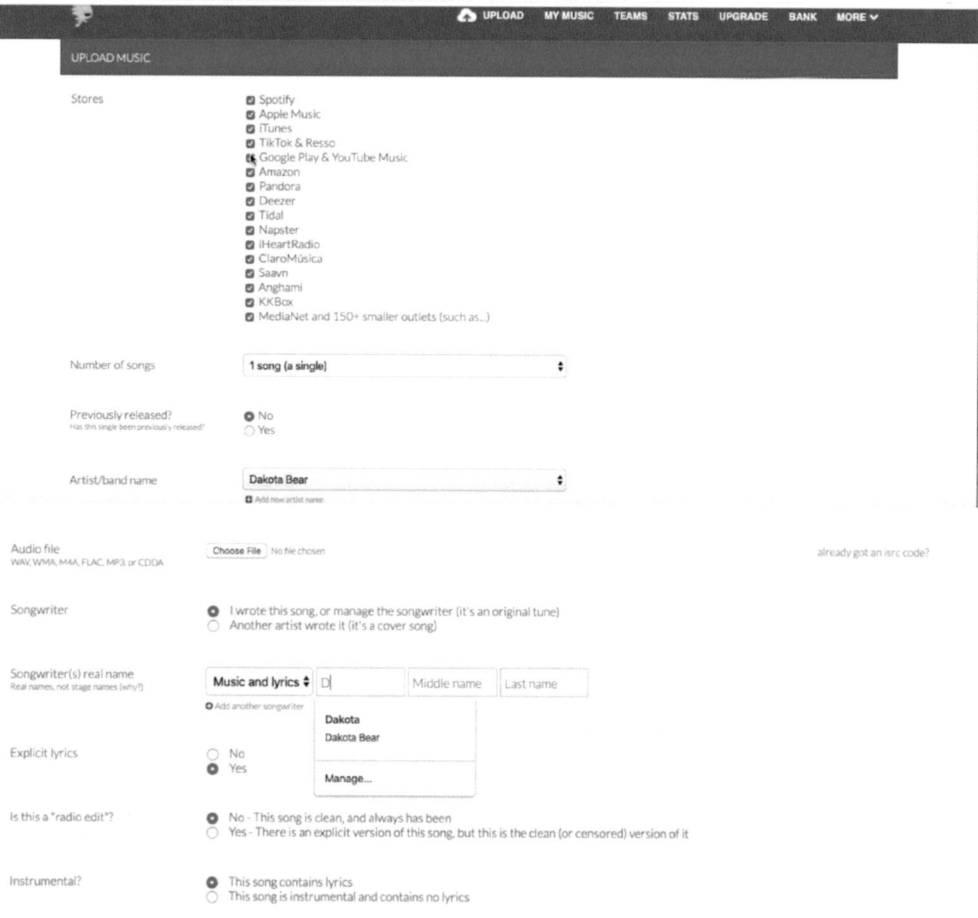

Upload your artwork and set the language of your music.

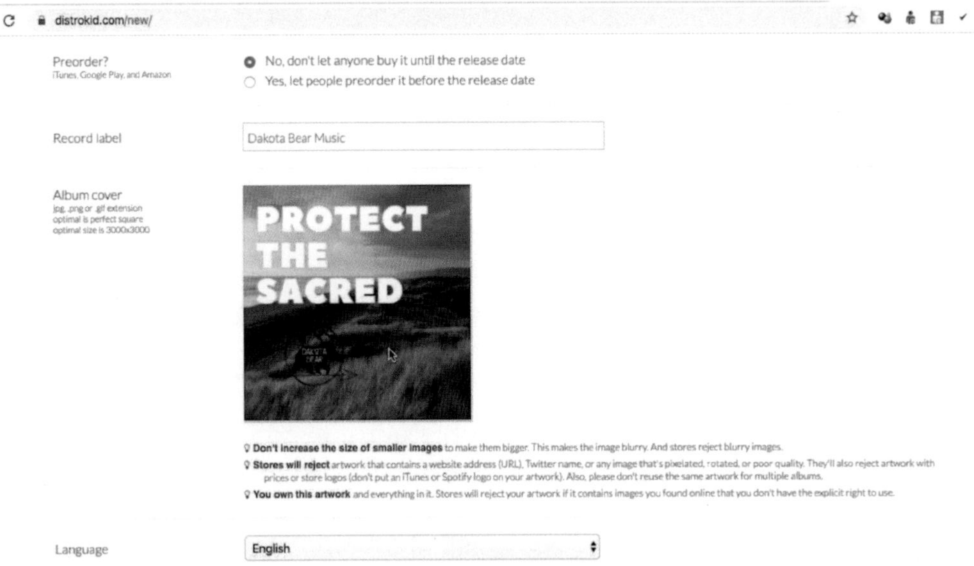

Select your genre and enter your song title.

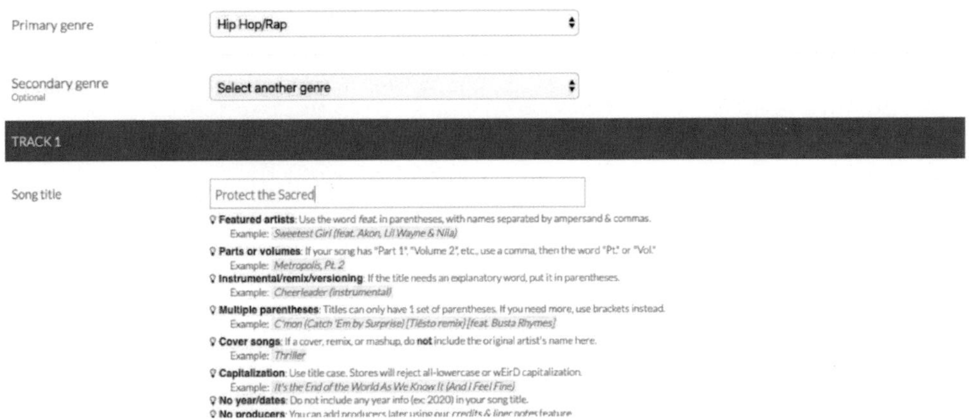

Upload your audio file, identify if you wrote the song, and enter who wrote the music and lyrics. Label it for explicit lyrics if applicable, if it's a radio edit and if it's an instrumental only.

Set where you want the preview to start and the price of your song.

Pick which extras you want, if you want to make a song available in stories and other options.

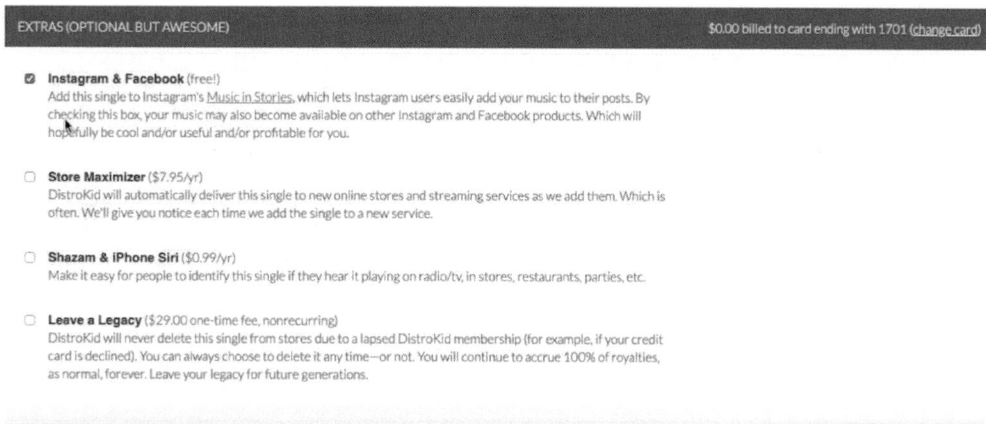

Go through the mandatory checklist and hit “done”.

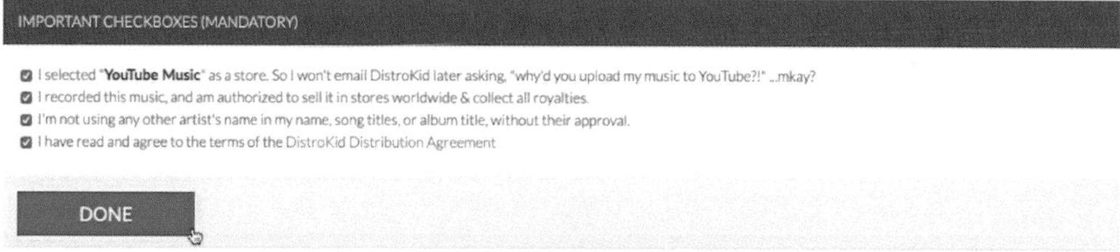

You’ve uploaded your first single! Congratulations! It takes a few weeks to get your song visible in stores. Make sure your release date is at least a week out to maximize your opportunity to get added to playlists. Now, go get more music out there!

LESSON 7: PRESS AND PUBLICITY

> *“It’s all about persistence. It’s all about determination, how bad that you want people to get your music, listen to your music, review it.”*

In this lesson we will be talking about press and publicity, which is very important as a musician. We can spend time on our craft, perfecting our melodies and our flows. But if we’re wanting to pursue this into the music industry, then we need to know who we have to reach and how do we get our music out there?

You're going to need these tools to get noticed:

- A bio
- EPK
- Headshots
- Press Release

Once you create all of these things, you're going to want to source out some people to start sending your music and these materials to, like:

- Magazines
- Newspapers
- Blogs
- Reviewers

You're going to want to send your bio and all of those communications assets in a link to try and get featured. A couple examples Dakota provided were Exclaim and Hiphop Canada. Outreach takes consistency and dedication.

TIPS:

- You can hire out your bio creation to someone, but you can also do it yourself to save money.
- Your press release should have information on what you're trying to promote.

How to do Outreach

- Customize each outreach email. Find an editor or writer and use their first name.
- Send them an email about your song with attachments.
- Read up on their work.
- Mention the things that you liked and you've seen in their work.

Getting Heard

If you're wanting to do radio, it's a similar process. You have to put together an online radio package and then send it out to different online or college radio stations. If you're an indigenous artist, there are about 3000 Indigenous communities in Canada alone. The majority of them have radio stations.

> *"I think that's important as an artist that we're spending just as much time on the business side as we are on the music side, because we can produce music, we can write our songs and do our art, but if we're really wanting to pursue it in the music industry, then we're going to have to start learning the business."*

MUSIC INDUSTRY SKILLS AS TRANSFERABLE SKILLS

The basics of business within the music industry and these skills, this knowledge and insights can apply to many different things. You can apply it within your business to get articles and write-ups for new businesses that you're launching.

Here's an example of Dakota's bio:

ARTIST BIO

Dakota Bear is a Saskatoon-born, Vancouver-based Indigenous hip-hop artist and activist. His melodic rhymes carry stories of Indigenous peoples across Canada leaving listeners enlightened, inspired and instant fans of his music and message. His performances range from audiences of 30,000 (Global Climate Strike with Greta Thunberg, Downtown Vancouver, October 2019) to inspirational performances for youth in remote communities in Northern Canada. His work with Idle No More, Missing and Murdered Indigenous Women, Girls and Two-Spirited Peoples and the Global Climate Strike movement has intertwined his music with international social justice movements and connected him with fans across the country. He's shared stages with legendary greats like Bone Thugs n Harmony, Redman & Methodman, TechN9ne and more. His music has been shared by Noisey, Exclaim!, Hip Hop Canada, Digital Drum and numerous grassroots-news outlets while his online videos have collectively amassed more than 1 million views. His quest for love, justice and peace is unwavering, with his melodic rhymes and iconic beats carrying his message to the masses and beyond.

Live Different Youth Empowerment Tour 2019

Edmonton, AB - John D. Bracco Junior High School
Glenvis, AB - Alexis Nakota Sioux Jr./Sr. High School
Duncan, BC - Quamichan Middle School

The bio will include:

- Your name
- Where you're from
- Where you're based out of
- Talk about my performances
- Press you've had

A good bio is something that you're going to need when you're doing applications for festivals and you're doing your press. Check out Dakota's website for a full example.

Press Release

Dakk'One
30604 Music

Dark City 3 - *The Storm Is Coming*

Dakota's press release has a stunning visual component, it says it's for Immediate Release, and includes his name. Search on Google how to write a press release, but here is an example of what Dakota included in his:

Vancouver-Based Hip-hop Artist Dakk'One releases powerful new visual to promote his upcoming EP

The Saskatoon raised artist is back with video director **Fremo Skillz** with the third installment to the "Dark City" series, and it's the most impactful yet. Over the ominous but uptempo production **Dakk** touches on many hardships his community faces including poverty, gang violence and domestic abuse. **Dakk** exposes the mainstream glorification of violence and drug abuse that he can relate to his own life stories and others around him. "At the end of the day it's all glorified I was a youngin when I seen my momma clinging to life on a hospital bed I was horrified" he raps as he visits a childhood memory. Highlighting the police brutality and what was once known as the Starlight Tours, **Dakk** shines a light on the dark history of the death of 17-year-old Neil Stonechild that was once erased from the Saskatoon Police Services wikipedia page. **Dakk** is aware that events like these are still happening today and the only way to stop the violence is promoting the strength of his culture, acknowledging the faults of the system and working towards real reconciliation that he believes will be Indigenous-led. "Dark city 3" is promoting **Dakk'One's** forthcoming effort titled *The Storm Is Coming* a 5 song EP set to release July 1st, Canada Day via all streaming platforms.

Watch "Dark City 3" here
https://www.youtube.com/watch?v=R2rMy2AWoqk&feature=youtu.be
Social Media
Facebook

Make sure to include your social media handles and your contact information so people can get in touch with you.

Electronic Press Kit

The electronic press kit is what you're going to send out to the press, to the media, and to radio stations. It should include your social links, information about you, highlight performances, pictures of you, your logo, project releases, quotes about your work, your contact information and that of your publicist, and your website.

About the Artist

Dakota Bear; formally known as Dakk'One, is an Indigenous hip-hop artist and activist based out of Vancouver, BC. Dakota has been using his platform to raise awareness and drive change within his community. Through his music he spreads an empowering message. He has the potential to open minds and inspire many.

Mission and Vision

Dakk'One has set out to strengthen the identity of his Indigenous culture. He's aware of the plight his people face and has made his mission to use his platform to educate and promote healing to others. With the power of social media he is determined to create a youth-led movement that will make changes for the next wave of young minds.

- TechN9ne
- BC Youth in Care Week
- Stache 4 Cash Fundraiser
- Connected North Fundraiser
- National Indigenous Day
- Sofar Sounds
- Simon Fraser University
- University of British Colombia
- Create 2 Learn Youth Summit
- Global Youth Service Summit
- (Featuring Greta Thunberg)
- Hiphop 4 Change

Radio

- CITR - FM
- MBC Radio
- CFRO - FM
- CBC Radio One
- CBC Reclaimed

- Hip Hop Canada
- Hip Hop Vancouver
- Exclaim!
- Dominionated
- La Presse
- Discorder Magazine
- BC Underground Hip Hop
- The StarPhoenix
- Saskatoon Express
- Georgia Straight
- Global News
- APTN National News

DAKOTA BEAR

- The Runway (2012)
- First Flight (2013)
- Fame or Destruction (2017)
- The Storm is Coming (2018)

- Dirty Laundry (2018)
- Dark City 3 (2018)
- Expire (2019)
- Freedom (2019)

"One listen-through of his low-key breakout single "Lullaby" and it is hard to deny the Vancouver-based rapper has something special. His delivery is raw but never overly aggressive. It has the emotional vulnerability characterized by a lot of the hip-hop coming out of Toronto, but thanks to the production on "Lullaby" and Dakk's skills as an MC, it feels fresher." - DOMINIONATED

WEBSITE

www.DakotaBear.ca

FREEDOM VIDEO

https://www.youtube.com/watch?time_continue=2&v=BdZJaxBybTA

CONTACT

janepuchniak@gmail.com
dakotabearmgmt@gmail.com

LESSON 8: REVENUE AND FUNDING

"As a musician, as an artist, myself, a hip hop artist, it's important to know where I'm going to be getting paid from. It's also important to know how I can access funding to launch some of my projects, because as an artist, a hip hop artist, there are so many costs for me."

In this lesson we are going to be talking about revenue streams and funding streams. Studio recordings and music videos cost money, though in the first year you won't have to worry about that.

REVENUE STREAMS:

Performances

You can make money off of your shows either through SOCAN (a publishing company) or by negotiating fees with the promoter.

Radio Play

Every time that your song gets played on the radio, SOCAN is going to bank some of that money for you. Then they're going to cut you a check and deliver the money that you're making off of your radio streams.

Merchandise

Learn how to silkscreen print yourself through YouTube tutorials. Get somebody to build you a screen.

Workshops and Speaking

Speak about and teach what you know as you become more advanced and have more to offer.

Distribution

Your distributor (Dakota uses DistroKid) will pay you for the number of times your songs are played online.

Grants

"Grant writing is extremely important."

Research what grants are available to you as an artist or Indigenous artist to support the costs of EPS, albums, music, and anything music business related.

Canada Council has a portal where, as an Indigenous person, you can access funds to start your album or your next short-term project. The smallest grant that they have is for $3,000 which can be helpful when you're recording an album or shooting a video.

Factor does grants for musicians who want to do albums.

With these funding sources, you'll be positioned to launch albums, videos and make a living off of your art. It will take commitment and determination, but you can achieve this if you want to.

"It'll take a little bit of time, but as long as you're determined, you're passionate, you know your goals, you know how you want to get there, it is very possible."

MOCCASIN MAKING

Carly Chartier

View the videos in this series online! Scan the QR code, or visit http://www.tigurl.org/moccasins

Carly Chartier is a Métis and Non-Status Youth located in Selkirk, Manitoba. Carly is a graduate of Red River College where she studied Human Resource Management, Management Development and graduated with honours. Carly is employed in her field of studies at The Selkirk Friendship Centre (a non-profit Indigenous organization) in Administration & Human Resources providing resources to her community. Carly is also a former community impact partner with the #RisingYouth program at TakingITGlobal.

PART 1

First, you're going to want to get together all the supplies to make the moccasins. You are going to need the leather/suede for the moccasin tops. You will want fleece liner to make them nice and cozy, some fur to keep them warm, a soft measuring tape, a needle for hand sewing and some thread to pull it all together.

Think about the strength and weight of the thread needed to support the weight of the fabrics and the amount of movement you make with your feet day to day. You're going to want to make sure that the stitching can stand up to regular wear and tear so you can create something that isn't just beautiful but is also highly functional. And remember, over time, the leather will stretch!

Take the fleecy fabric liner, fold it up and hand stitch it together.

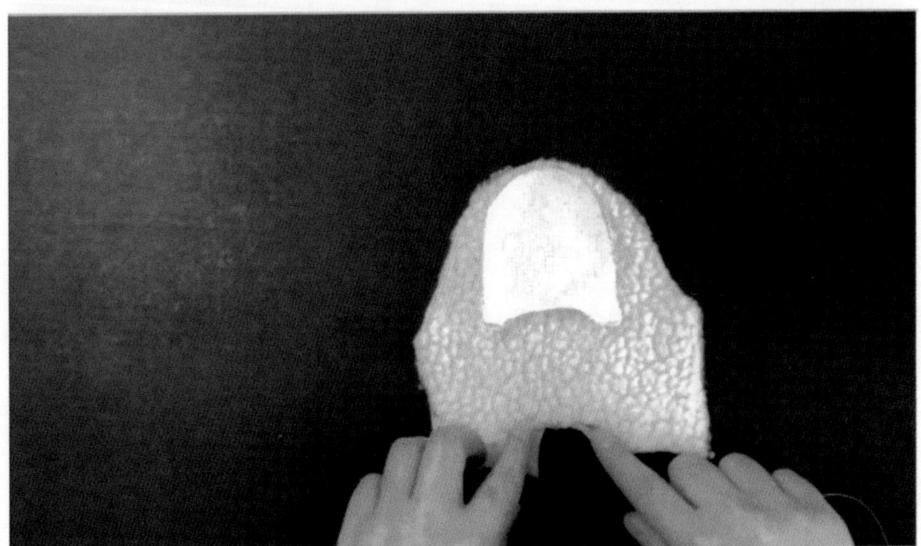

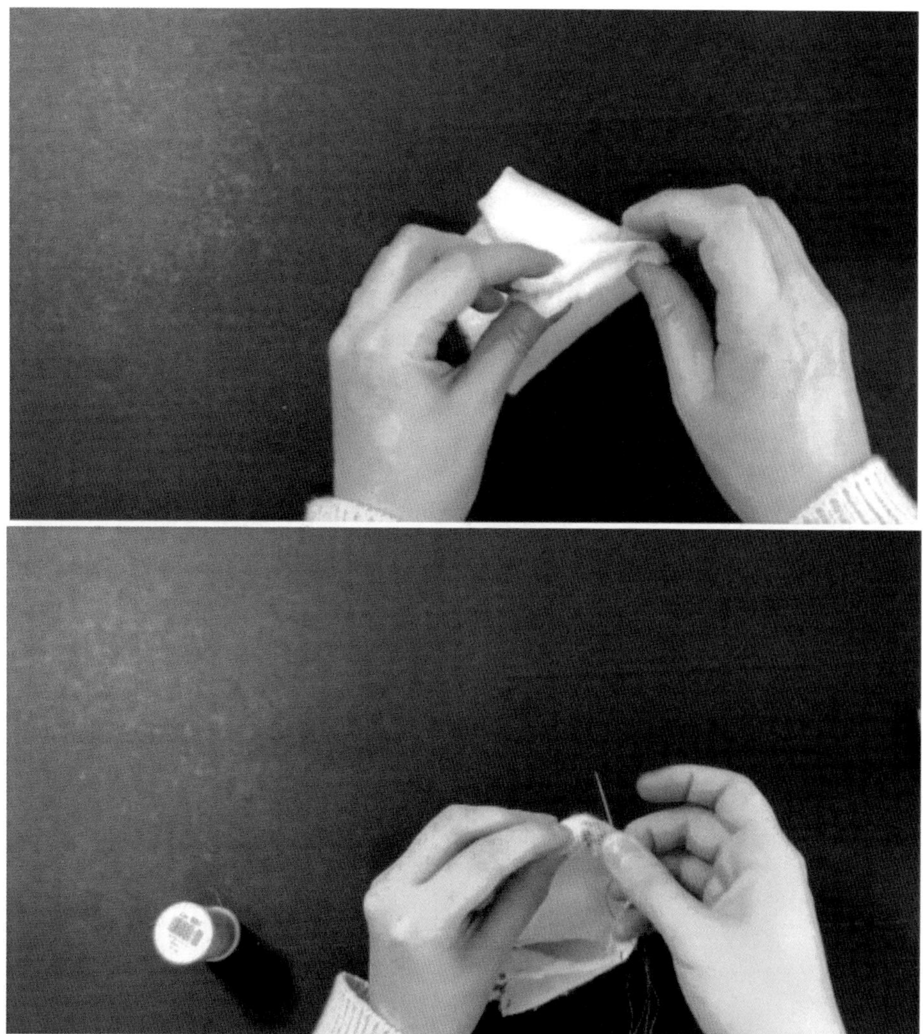

PART 2

Assemble the three pieces of suede-like material

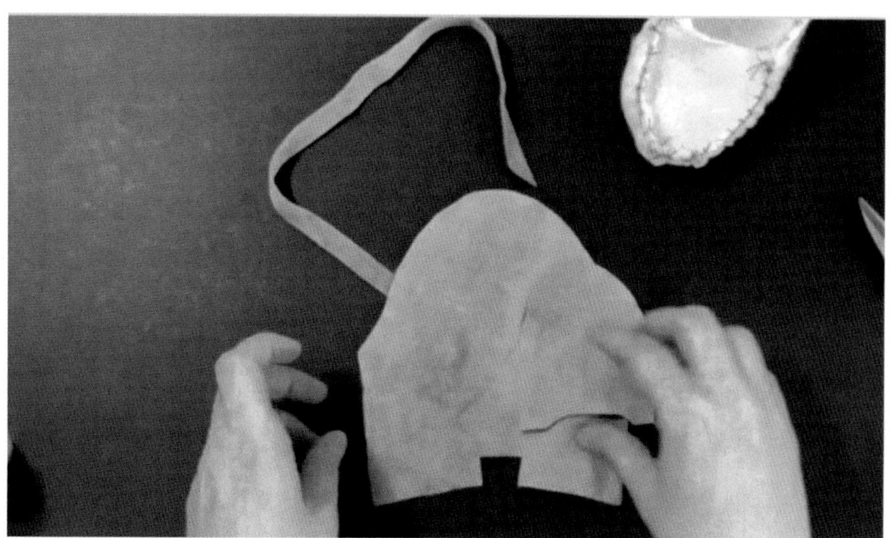

Stack them on top of each other.

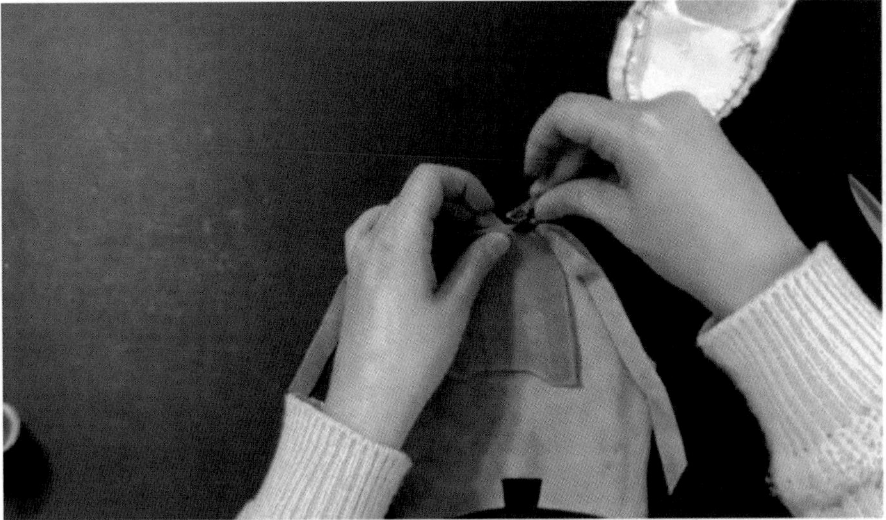

Pin the edges together.

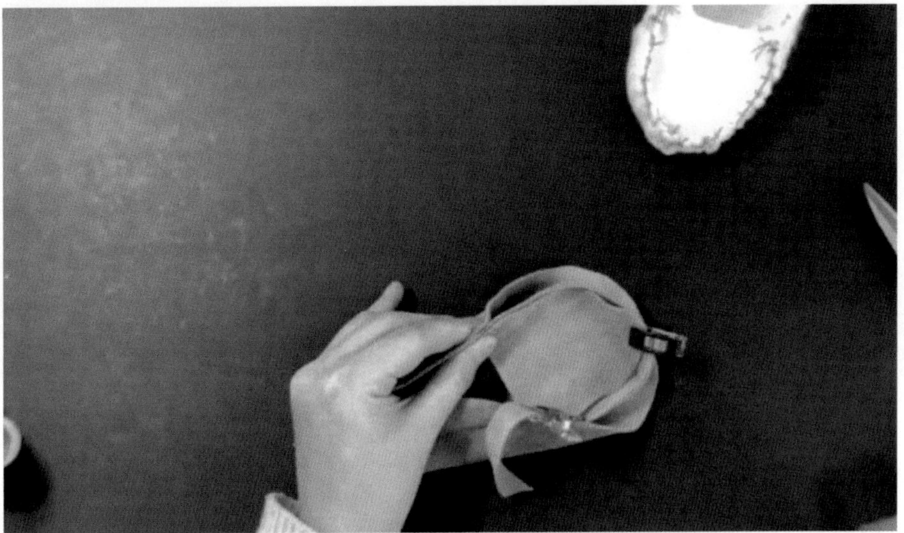

Stitch them together along the outside edges around the top.

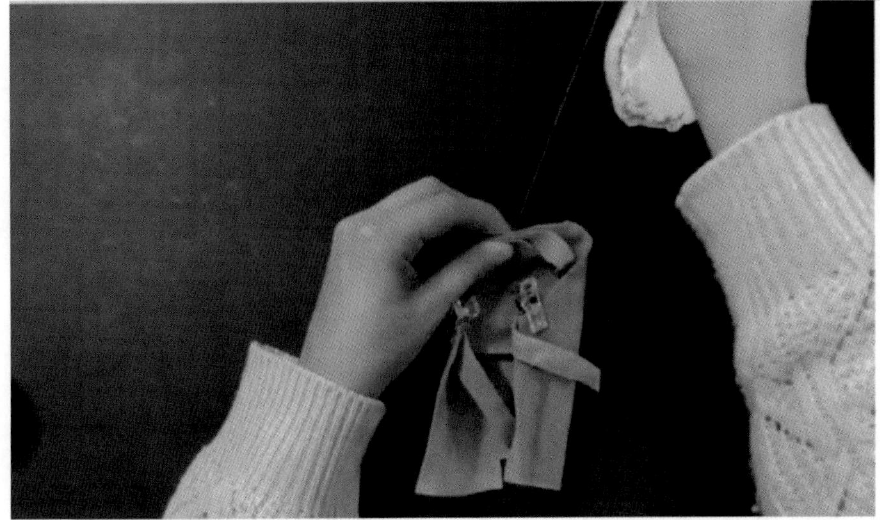

With your stitching you're going to create like a pouch that's open on the bottom.

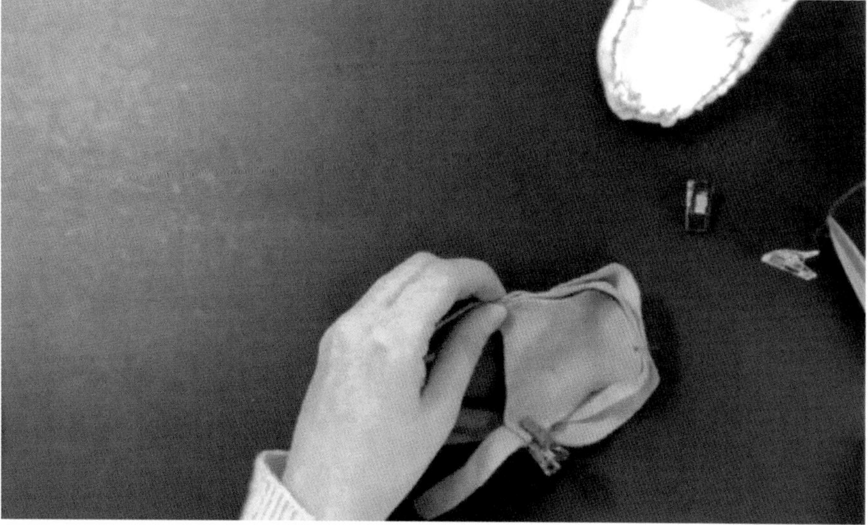

Then you will want to sew up that bottom edge.

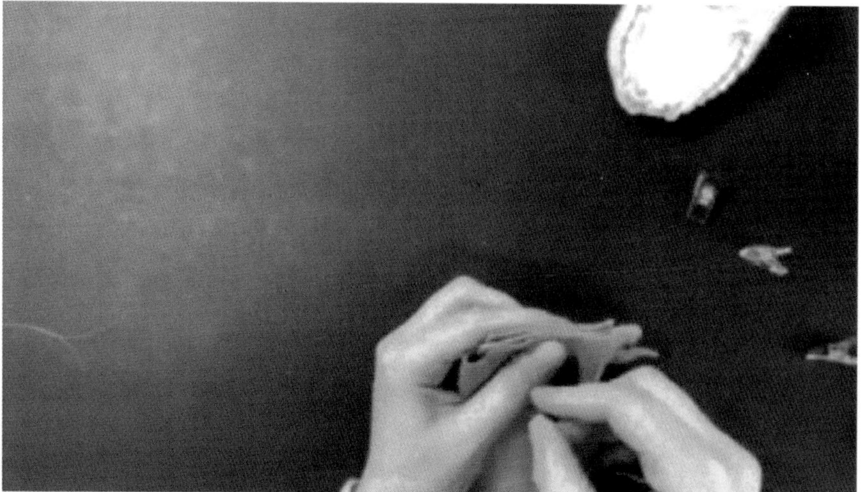

Stitch all the way around the outside.

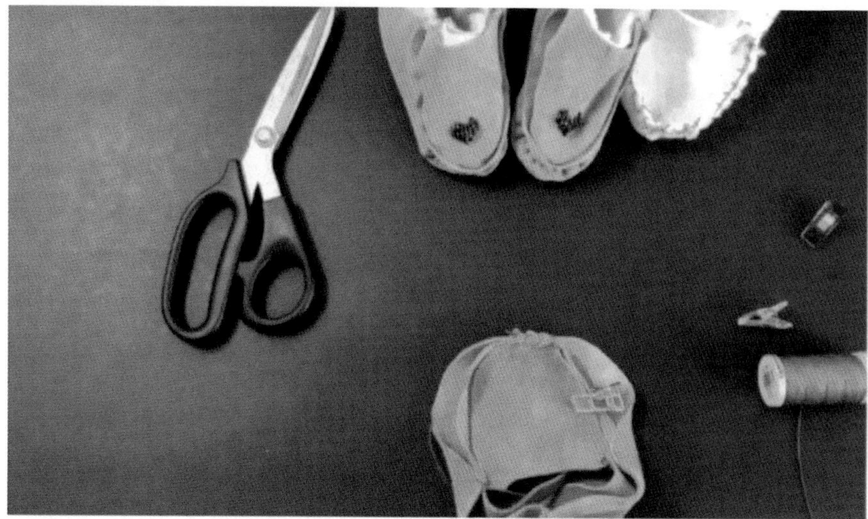

Keep stitching around the outside, leaving the centre flap open.

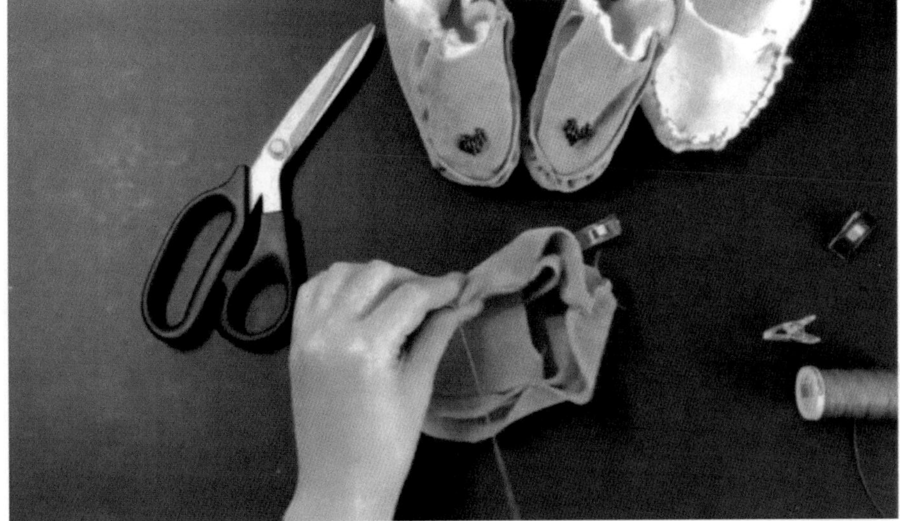

When you're working along the outside of the suede, it should look like this:

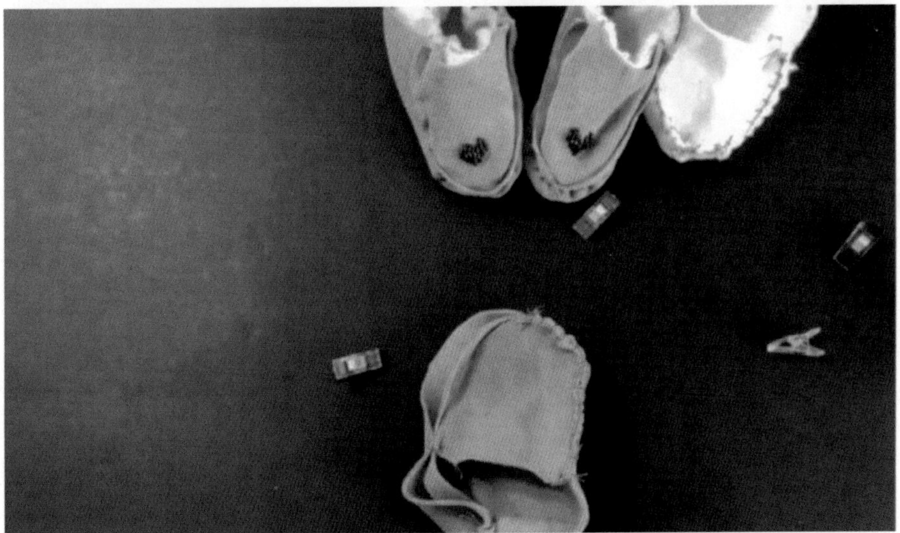

The tension of your stitches should make the outside edge pucker.

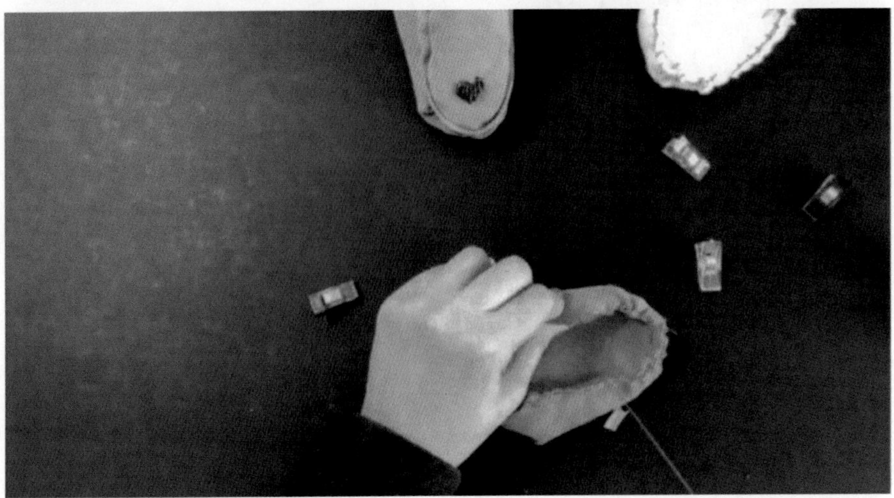

PART 3

Next, turn the suede inside out.

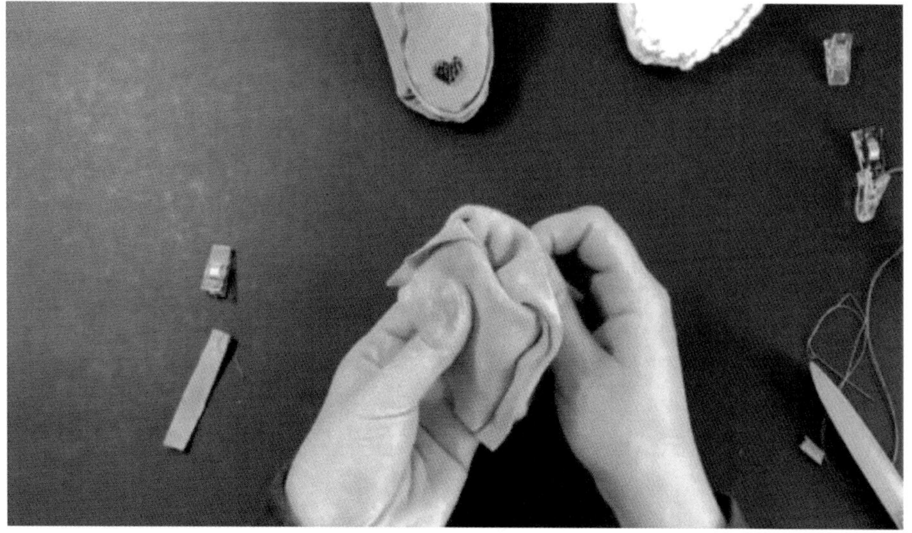

Cut any loose threads. Trim outside your stitches.

It should look like a neat pocket when it's trimmed up.

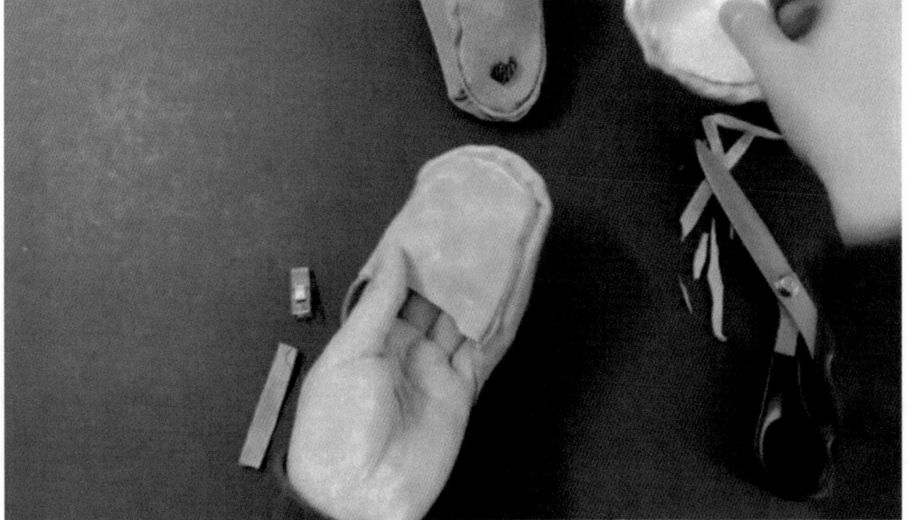

Place the fleece pocket into the suede pocket.

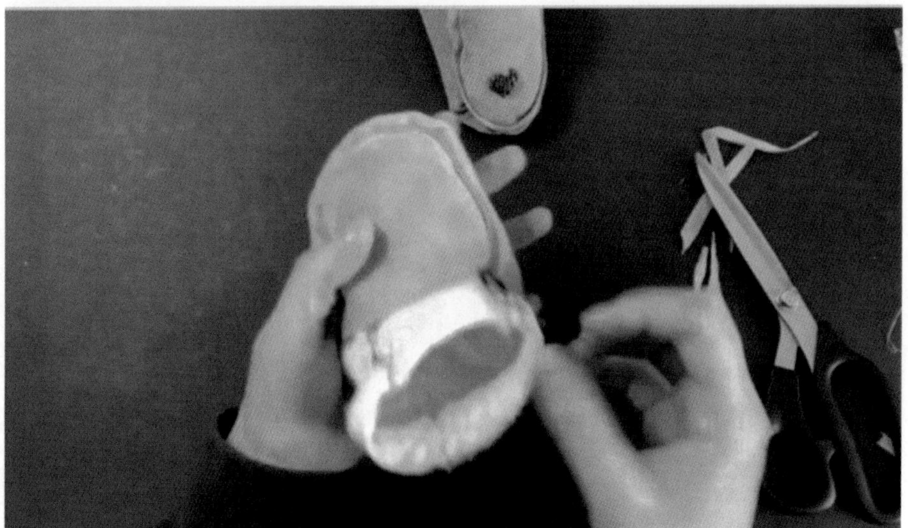

When one is inside the other it will look like this:

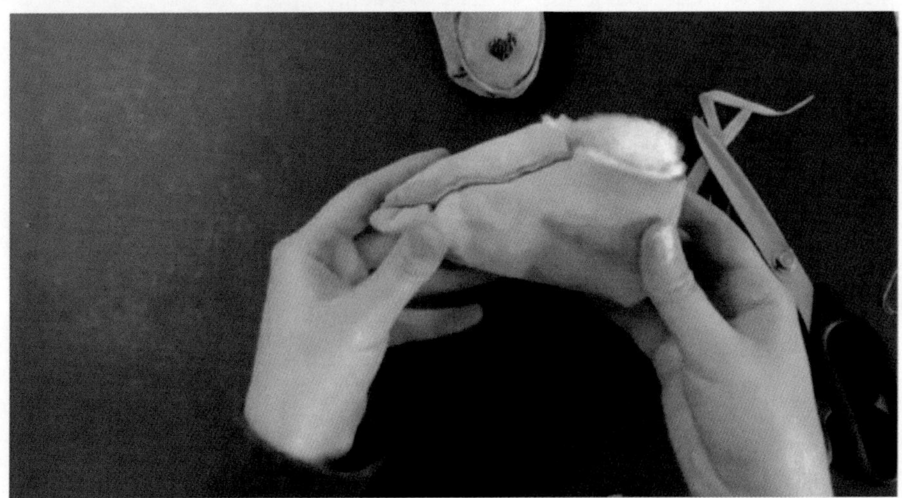

Stitch both layers together at the top.

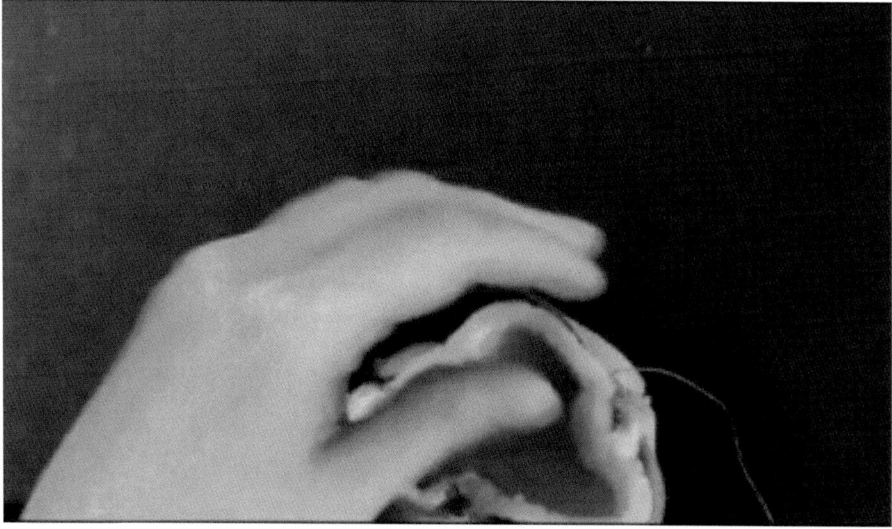

When stitched all the way around it should look like this:

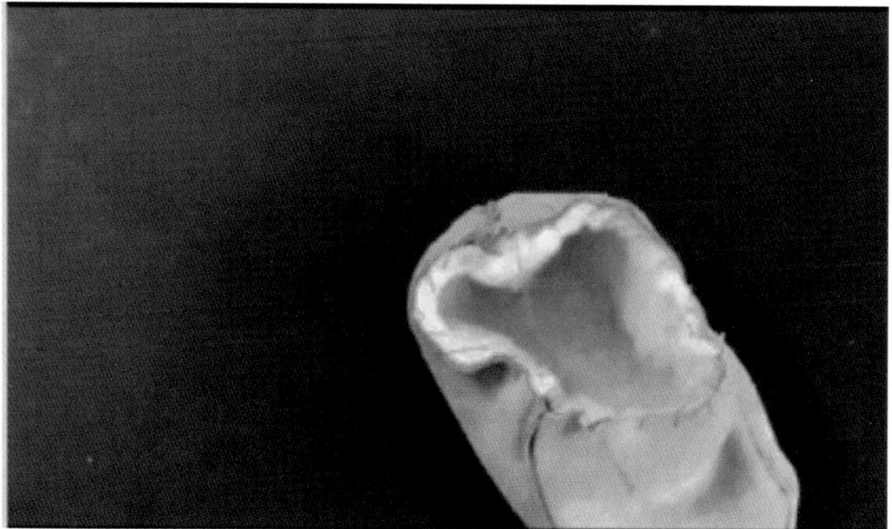

Your moccasin is starting to come together and take shape.

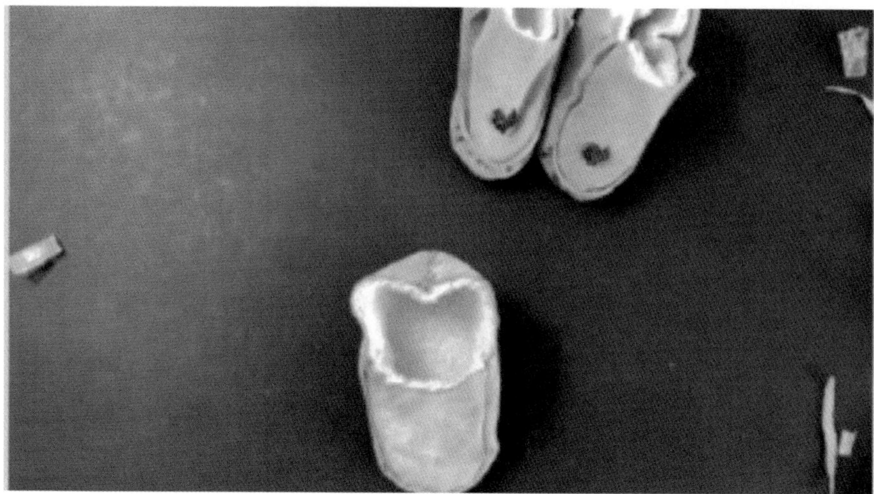

Measure the circumference of the opening.

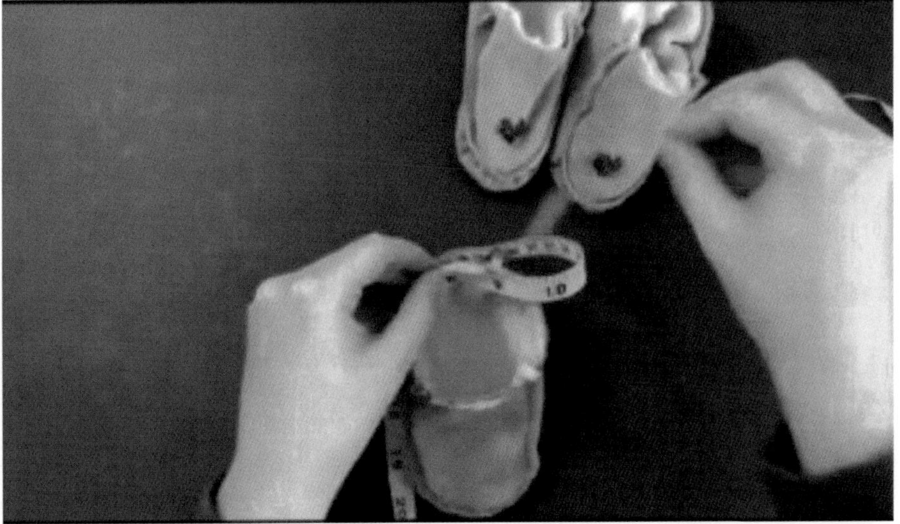

Measure the fur to match.

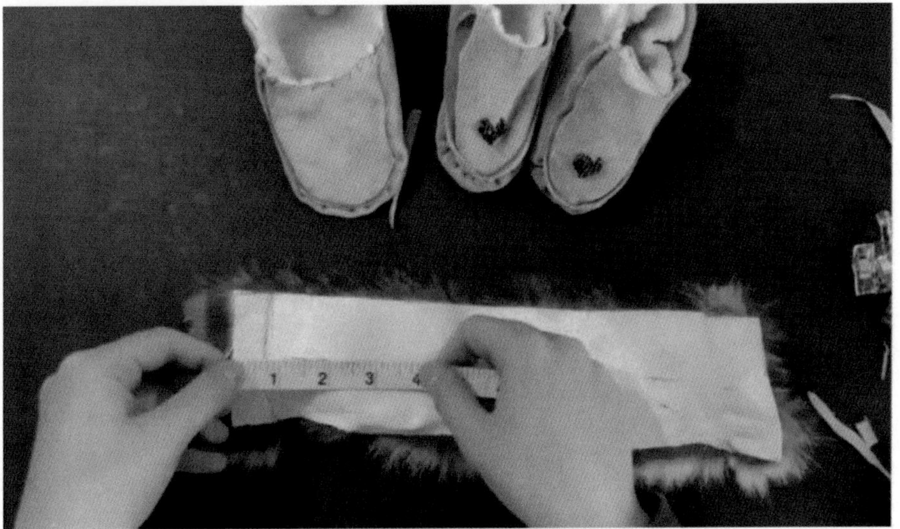

Mark out where you will need to cut the fur:

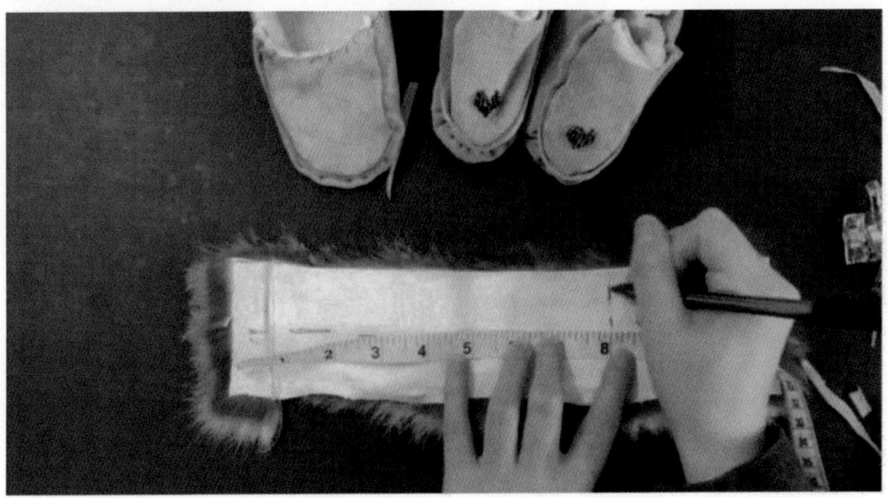

Cut along your markings with a knife. Do not use scissors as they will cut the fur and make it look choppy. You only want to cut the hide!

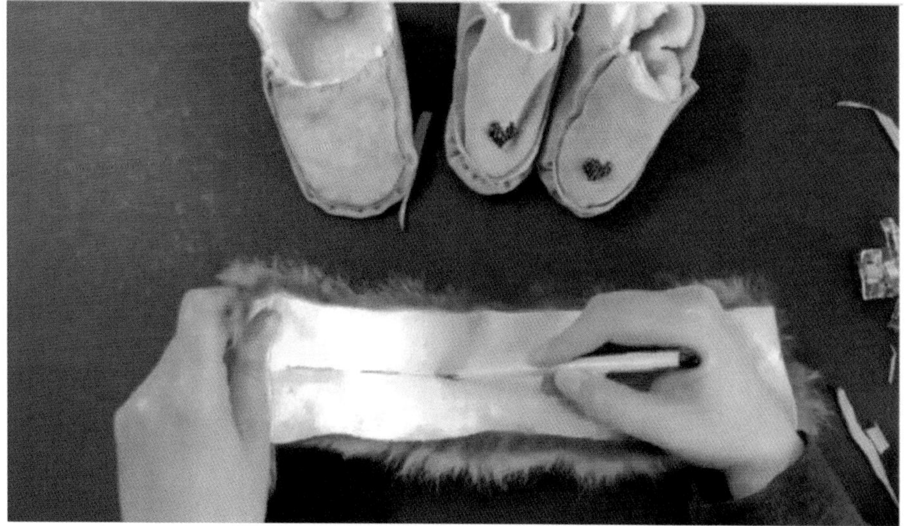

You will be left with a long thick strip of fur for your moccasin. '

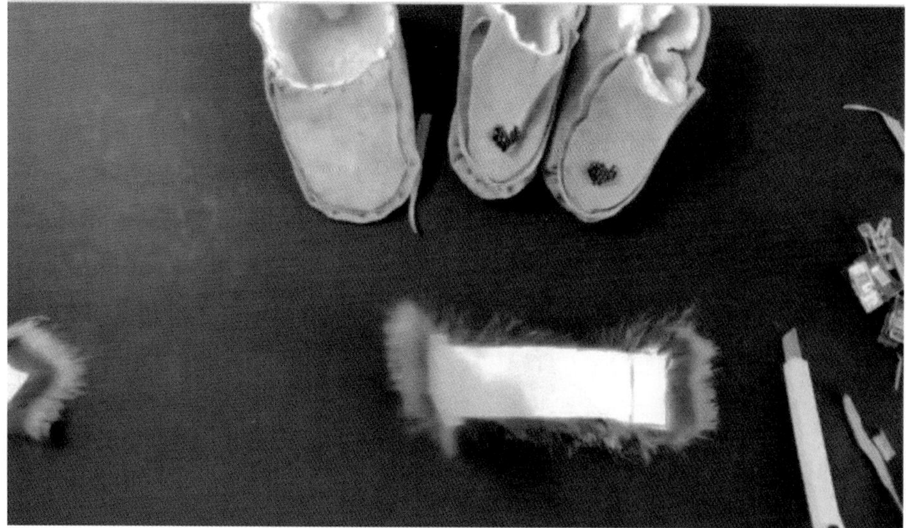

More of the pieces are ready to put together.

PART 4

Sew the fur to the backing.

Keep stitching along the edge.

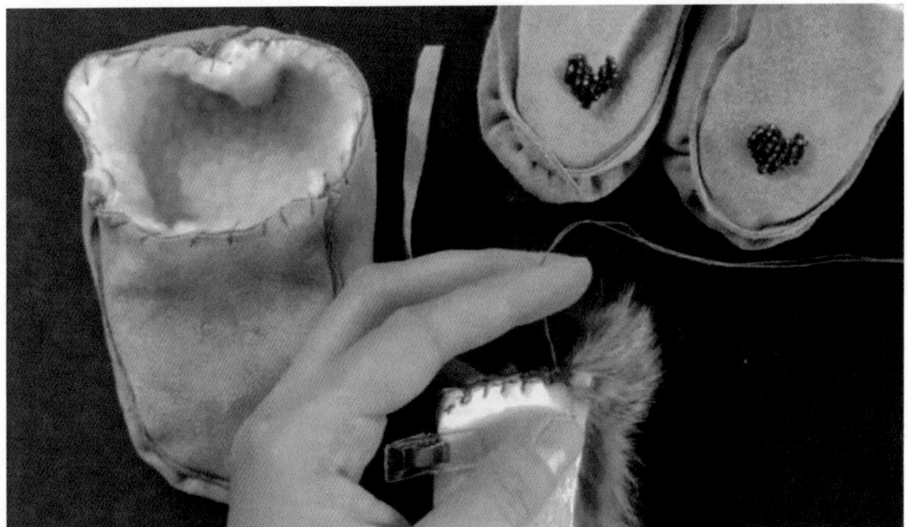

When that stitching is complete the fur and backing should make a circle.

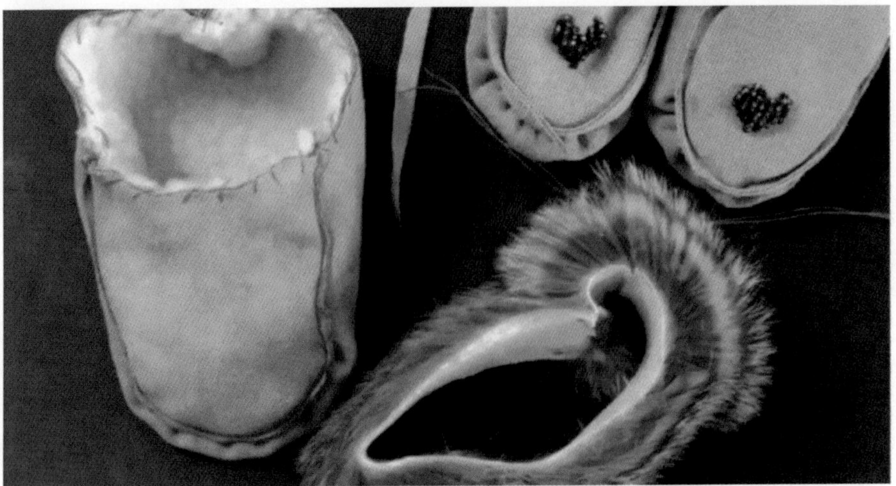

Sew the layers of the moccasin together around the top, the suede, the fleece and the fur.

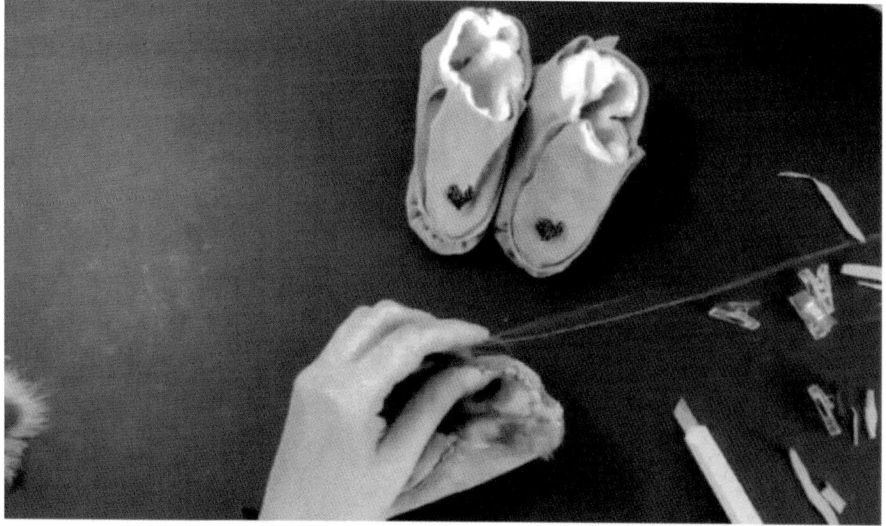

When you have sewed the moccasin layers together all the way around the top it will look like this:

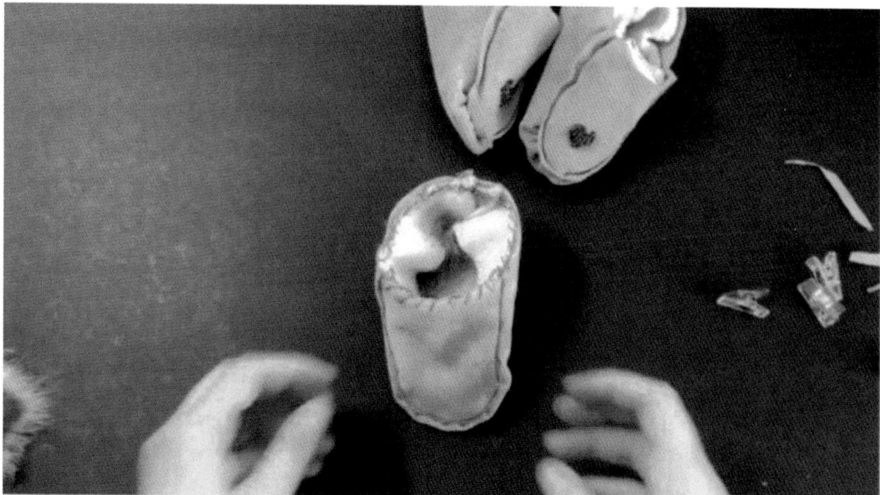

Pull the fur out from inside the moccasin:

When you've pulled it out, it will look like this:

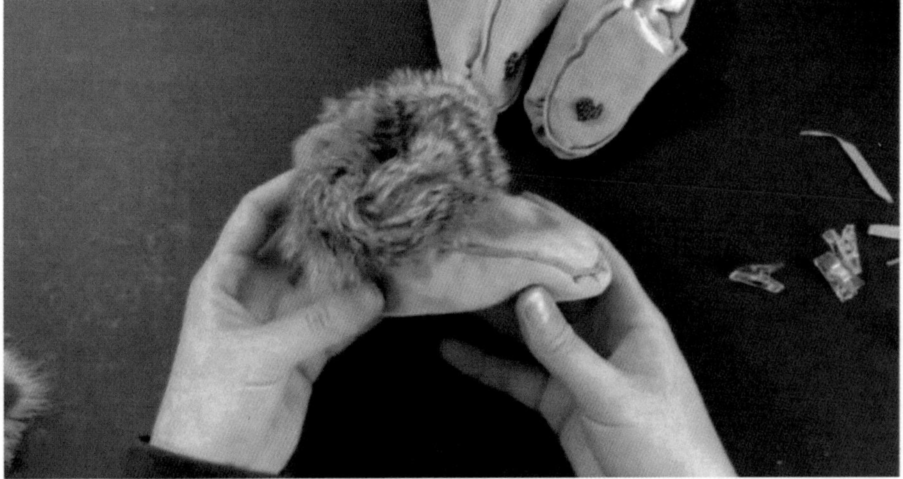

Congratulations, you've made a moccasin!

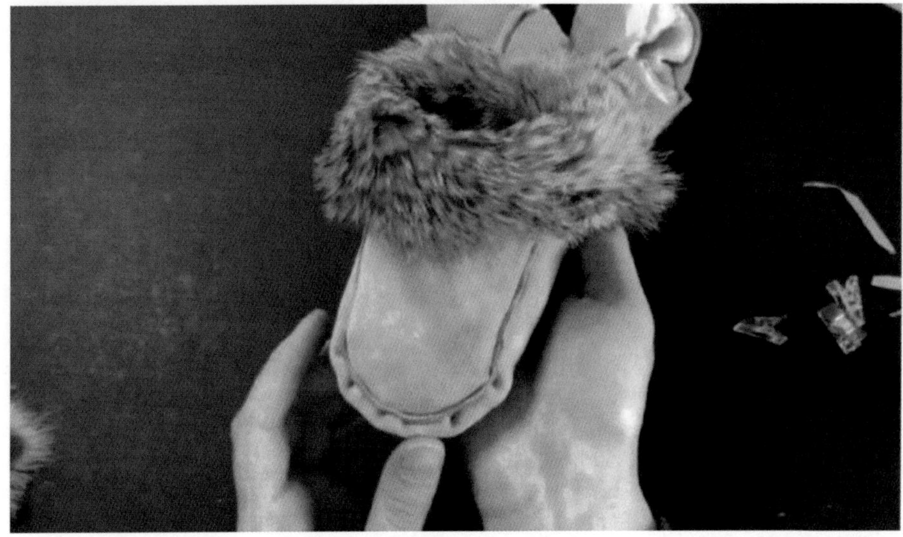

Want to take a closer look or get the things you need to make this project?

Go to Ambersleathercreations.com. Now you know how to make moccasins!

BEAUTY INDUSTRY WITH KRISTA PAUL

Krista Paul has a love for helping people both inside and out, and found it in the beauty industry. Born and raised in Saskatoon, Saskatchewan, she is a hairstylist and makeup artist and has been in the industry since 2009, changing and evolving throughout it all.

Paul went to cosmetology school for 10 months, where she learned things that she both expected and didn't expect.

"One of the things that I didn't really think of was the physiology of the body and understanding it and knowing it. So that was probably the hardest time in school," said Paul.

A lot of the focus was on hair but she also learned about makeup and "the basics of everything," but in doing so "you don't really get to know a whole lot."

So for the first five years of her career, Paul didn't take any extra education and worked at a salon to try and figure out what was next for her. Eventually, after staying at the same salon for a few years, Paul was questioning her career.

"I started to question whether or not I should still be doing hair because I just didn't have the spark anymore. I kind of felt like I kept doing the same thing over and over and over," said Paul.

She moved on to another salon and was introduced to more education about hair, taking a class about colour and learning more about it and "going back to the basics and fundamentals."

"That's when I was like, 'Oh, this is amazing,' because it just like reinvigorated my passion and it re-inspired me. So ever since then, I take so many education classes throughout the year."

Growing up Paul had no idea what she wanted to do or even if she wanted to be a hairstylist, she just remembers being young and cutting her friends bangs or styling their hair.

"I always had this little knack that I didn't think was part of my talent or you know what I naturally do," said Paul.

She also says people have assumptions about hairstyling saying it's fun she gets to "play with hair all day," but it's so much more than hair for her.

"One thing I always go back to is, I love helping people, but I get to help people on the outside and then on the inside," said Paul.

"That's why I became a hair stylist is because connecting with people and just making people feel their best."

Getting to where she is now wasn't easy. Paul says one of the things she had to face that was difficult was starting out and trying to figure out who exactly she was, because it's "what's going to drive you."

Another obstacle she faced was not being in the right environment where she could thrive.

"Sometimes you outgrow your environment depending on who you are because you change constantly," said Paul.

"Don't ever stay somewhere that doesn't make you feel good, or even in any other industry or career path you choose. If you don't feel good in that environment, find another environment that you can thrive because sometimes you outgrow it and sometimes you can keep growing."

SONG-WRITING 101

Evan Redsky

View the videos in this series online! Scan the QR code, or visit http://www.tigurl.org/songwriting

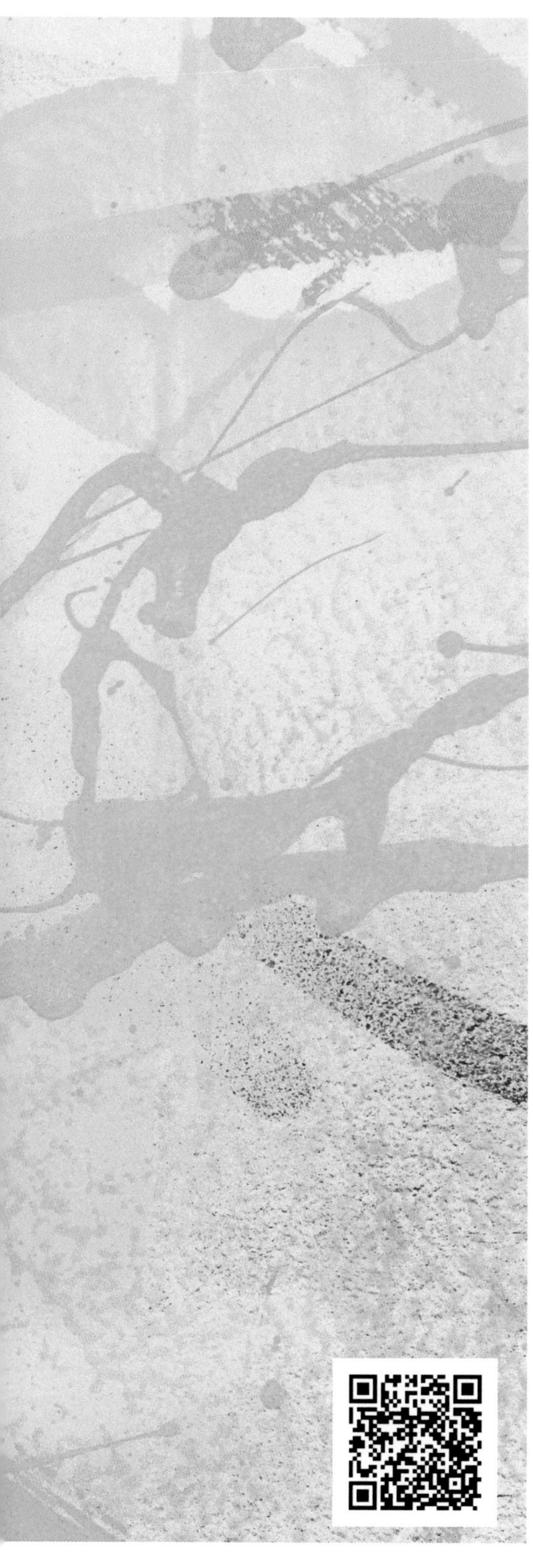

Evan Redsky is an Ojibway singer/songwriter from Blind River, ON. by way of Toronto. Having spent several years on the road with a Juno nominated rock and roll group - he has returned to his Indigenous storytelling roots. Painfully honest americana stories, straight from Canada's heartland.

LESSON ONE: FINDING INSPIRATION

"There's no right or wrong way to go about it. An idea for a song can strike you like a bolt of lightning."

COMING UP WITH AN IDEA OR CONCEPT FOR A SONG

Sometimes this can be the hardest thing and the hardest step of the process.

Ask yourself: What am I trying to communicate?

Is it a feeling? Are you happy? Are you sad? Are you melancholic? Are you angry?

"There's a technique to just opening up and looking for a line of something jumps out at you."

Choose your resources very wisely but theres are some places to find inspiration:

- Books
- Magazines
- Conversations with friends and family

"When you listen to people and you truly listen to people, they could say things that inspire you."

"Your writing is only as good as the books you read. Other people's language helps lift up your language"

INSPIRING PEOPLE AND THEIR BOOKS TO INSPIRE YOU:

- Waubshegig Rice - Moon of the Crusted Snow
- Tanya Talaga - All My Relations
- Billy Ray Belcourt (poet)
- Richard Wagames - Embers

"You never know what's going to be that bolt of lighting that sort of sets you on your path to telling your story, creating a narrative and ultimately writing a song."

Evan draws inspiration from this Toronto Hardcore book, an encyclopedia of punk rock in Toronto, Ontario since the late seventies, early eighties.

You can also find inspiration in art, like this Carl Beam book. Evan describes Carl as the grandfather of contemporary first nations art

"Writing within the indigenous community and being a part of the indigenous music community it's important to know all this stuff. It's important to help spread those stories."

Here is some music that inspires Evan:

- The Jayhawks *Rainy Day Music*
- Wilco *Sky Blue Sky*
- John Prine
- Lucinda Williams
- Gillian Welch *Soul Journey*

"You've got to have these tools to record these ideas."

TIPS:
- Keep a composition book or your cell phone on hand for lyrics and music memos.
- Revisit old ideas.

"There's never, ever, ever any bad ideas when it comes to songwriting and you should always be throwing paint at the wall."

LESSON 2 FINDING MORE INSPIRATION

"Some songs just happen and some songs just almost write themselves in a way."

When writing Time Bomb, Evan was inspired by Tania's writing about the challenges Indigenous people face. He encourages aspiring songwriters to draw inspirations from anywhere and everywhere and to be aware that these won't always be happy things but it's important to share your perspective.

"The important part of this whole process is that you're always listening with an open heart to literally anything."

Being open to the inspiration around you is so important as a songwriter. You might feel like you look crazy talking into your phone on the street to record an idea, but it's worth it.

"Inspiration can literally quite literally just be anywhere and fall from the sky. If you always pick up those pieces and you put them in your back pocket, so to speak, you just never know when it can inspire you to just finish and write a song."

We are always having experiences and things are always happening around us. All of these experiences can become songs. A good song can be about anything, even your pets.

"As an early songwriter, I encourage you to write about absolutely anything and to get all those ideas down, because your first song is not going to be the best song you write.

TIPS:

- Look for ways to weave things you love into your music
- Meet new people
- Explore art galleries
- Gather more sources of inspiration and get ready to get inspired!

LESSON 3: NARRATIVE

"That's important in any narrative, in any story that you tell us to choose specifically, who is saying what?"

Evan had the idea for a few lines of a song, the chorus and the chords so he came home and started putting it together. He played with musical ideas to help create the music for his song.

In building the song, he was shaping the narrative as he went. He decided to write from a "we" perspective instead of a first person perspective.

"I think the first line should draw not only draw the listener in, but it should set up that point of view. When you're throwing ideas at the wall, you should really narrow in on a perspective. When it comes to songwriting specificity, in my opinion, is key to drawing out a narrative."

ACCESSIBILITY AND NARRATIVE

Evan encourages songwriters to write in a more general way to be more palatable. He cautions that going too specific or too personal can alienate potential listeners. He likens it to taking an old Folk music perspective of togetherness to speak to issues as a society vs as an individual in society.

Tip: The chorus should be the most exciting part of the song. It should be the part of the song that stands out and is catchy.

LESSON 4: BREAKING DOWN LYRICS

"I think you should really come sort of locked and loaded when it comes to not only topical music, like political songs, protest songs, but I was just really proud of how all of those words got me to the first chorus, because it builds up a tension and it builds up this anxious feeling, the feeling of the pains of futility."

HOW EVAN WORKS WITH LYRICS

"Some people have the idea that you're born with talent when really it's just chipping away. It's all about just rolling up your sleeves and chipping away at the song."

Evan explains how the trickiest part of any song is writing that first verse that just really sets up the tune and gets you to that first chorus. If you have all the right ingredients, the chorus is just that much better.

What about rhyming? Evan says "It's nice to rhyme. It's pleasing to the listener. It's pleasing on the ears."

BREAKING DOWN STANZAS AND RHYME

Evan breaks down the lyrics of his song. He labels the similar lines A and B to show how he has created the rhymes. He doesn't go for obvious rhymes so he can avoid cliches. His first verse is broken down accordingly as A, A, B, B. He varies this for his next verse. As for the instrumental, he chose chords that were similar to the chorus but in a different pattern.

"There's no hard and fast rule. I just think that when you write a verse, it should stick to some structure."

LESSON 5: ARRANGEMENT

"There's no rules to writing music or writing songs, but it makes the job easier when you have a loose set of rules or a guideline to follow."

When it comes to music, whether it's pop music, punk, music, even classical music, any type of genre of music is going to have an arrangement. In the same way that storytelling has a structure, a beginning, middle and end with a climax, arrangements of music typically have an intro, verse, chorus, maybe a bridge, and then another chorus. These elements help package your story and move your narrative forward.

PULLING IT ALL TOGETHER

Evan's songs typically follow a formula.

Intro

The introduction introduces the listener to the music, the key of the song, the sort of overall feeling the vibe with the chords you've chosen.

After a few bars, you can start into your first verse.

Your verse is really where the meat of your song is. That's where you get your point across - within the two to three verses in a three to five minute pop song or folk song or a rock song. That's your storytelling section

Then the Chorus, the catchy big message that everybody can sing along to is generally what ties the theme of the song together. This is the essence of the song.

Then there's Verse 2, where you push your narrative, you push your story, you take the story to the next level. Your second verse should echo your first in terms of the narrative perspective (I or We.)

Next is the Chorus again and then the bridge. The bridge is either a musical break or another section of the song that's different. It usually has a little higher energy or completely stripped back energy where you can say a little bit more.

Finally, we move back into the chorus, because people are already singing along and humming to it. You can end with the first couple lines of the song, but the chorus is a great way to close out a song.

THE VALUE OF SIMPLICITY
However you arrange things, keep it simple.

> *"The best songwriters are able to get their point across and really distill their message in as [few] words as possible."*

Now that you know how to arrange a song, you can start giving your ideas a more defined shape!

LESSON 6: THE GUITAR

For this lesson, your guitar should be tuned with a standard E, A, D, G, B, E.

You can add different effects to your guitar play either through strumming or picking. In the example Evan shared with us, he was playing the verse chords without any vocals. This gave him space to add embellishments that would be harder to pull off while singing.

Working with the dynamic and the space in the music can help break up repetition. By adding flourishes, you're giving the song more life so you can start telling the story.

Tune into Evan's video and play along! '

LESSON 7: HOME STUDIO SETUP

Evan shared with us his home studio set up to give a behind the scenes look at his process. It has a piano, guitar, and a dynamic microphone.

The microphone is used typically for broadcasting and voiceover work. Evan finds it works well for recording vocals and voices.

He uses a pop filter to help pick up P's, T's and S's. Before he could afford a pop filter he used his mom's old nylons.

A condenser microphone is much more refined. They are slightly more expensive than a dynamic microphone and really sensitive. It does require a little bit more in the way of power, but it picks up all the really fine details in recording. It's good for detailed vocals and acoustic guitar.

Next up are recording interfaces which give you a slightly more polished end result. They start at a couple to a few hundred dollars. They are nice to have but not necessary.

GETTING STARTED

When you're just getting started, you don't need all this gear and you don't need all these sort of technical things to produce your demo. You could use something as simple as your phone. Garageband and Music Memos will do a great job of recording your music.

Microphone Placements

Your phone has a little microphone in it, and that's how it's going to pick up the sound. Whether you're using Garageband or Music Memos (both free apps you can get on your app store), there are a couple things to keep in mind.

- Good mic placement helps you record clear and detailed sound information.

- Don't put it on your lap next to your guitar. It will sound all boom-y and distorted. Your voice won't be audible.

- Don't put it in your pocket aimed up at your mouth or it will be too close.

- Put your microphone on a surface or stand a foot away, pointed between your guitar and your voice. Turn your guitar away a bit and keep your voice directed at the mic. You will want to make sure it's far enough away that you won't distort the microphone and you won't get a bad sounding recording, but you'll get something that's clear that'll get the guitar and the voice. Recording a quality demo doesn't need fancy expensive apps, it just needs good mic placement.

In terms of what kind of mic to use, a stage microphone is one you sing into and it will pick up most things without getting boomy or distorted.

Alternatively, this style of microphone is really good at picking up acoustic guitar, because it's more sensitive and picks up more detailed sound information.

When you're recording both vocals and instrumentals at the same time, sing directly into the microphone recording your vocals and point the other microphone towards the middle of your guitar and place it a little further away than your vocal mic.

Proper mic placement gives you more options for post-production mixing. You can mix in other instruments or vocals from collaborators to round out your sound and make music with your friends and family. With these tips, recording a demo of your song doesn't have to be complicated and you don't need a lot of expensive equipment to get started. Good luck making your demo!

LESSON 8

Evan was part of a band called Single Mothers which was signed to a record label called XL recordings. He and his band recorded an album and travelled the world performing music, which he considered to be an amazing feat as a kid from a small reserve in Northern Ontario. They recorded a 12 inch LP in Los Angeles, California.

He loves engaging with emerging artists and welcomes people to reach out to him to discuss music and songwriting and breaking into the industry. With these insights, you should be able to get a start on writing your first song.

FILM AND PHOTO GRAPHY BASICS

Sara Cornthwaite

View the videos in this series online! Scan the QR code, or visit http://www.tigurl.org/fpbasics

Sara Cornthwaite has worked in the film industry from documentary work to broadcast work, to editing, to animating, to voiceover works, photography works. She is from Nipissing First Nation in North Bay, Ontario. Her series focuses on how to use film and how to do it with a small budget, how to be creative, how to be crafty and how that's helped her throughout her 10 years of working in film.

LESSON 1: RULE OF THIRDS

The first concept Sara talks about is the Rule of Thirds. It's a guideline for composing visual images.

Start with imagining there is a grid on your camera that looks like this:

That grid is applicable no matter which way you flip your camera.

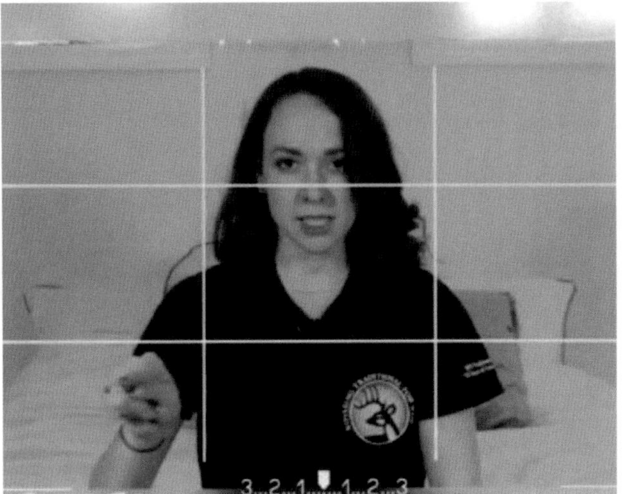

This is how the grid looks on an actual image.

You always want two thirds of your image to be one element and one third to be another. That could be two thirds of your image being a person and a third being your background or vice versa. You're also going to want to check your alignment to make sure your image isn't twisted or crooked.

With the right angles and while considering the rule of thirds, you can create compelling film captures of the world around you. Keep these composition tips in mind and go be fearless!

LESSON 2: EXPOSURE

Sara's second lesson is about exposure. To start, she explains the concepts of aperture, shutter and ISO.

This is how she explains aperture:

Think of it like an eyeball. When you're looking at the sun, your pupils physically get really, really small. When you turn back and you're looking at a more neutral, darker setting, your irises are going to open up that much more and let that light back. When your aperture is as open as it can be you're creating a really, really, really shallow focus.

Sara likes to keep her aperture at 2.8 and that means that there's just a little bit of space for your camera to recognize things and focus and everything else around will be blurred. Alternately, with an aperture of 11, 20 or 22, you're able to see everything in focus around it. She finds 2.8 ideal for storytelling because it helps her focus on people, smiles, objects, and details.

"I'm often trying to pull attention to one thing. I think people probably love the aperture open photos the most too, just because you get blurred stuff around and it looks really beautiful."

Shutter speed is how fast your shutter in the camera is going to close and open in a second. In that second of it being up and down, light is being let in. Your shutter speed,

whether fast or slow, controls how much time the light hits your sensor.

If you're filming somewhere really, really bright, you want a fast shutter speed because you don't need a lot of light. If the shutter is open too long, your photo will become overexposed. If the place you are filming is really dark, the opposite is true.

If you want to capture something fleeting, like droplets in the air, fast shutter speed is important so the image isn't just a blur.

Night exposure uses a slow shutter speed, where the shutter is open anywhere from 10 seconds to 30 seconds. The light from the star needs enough time to embed on your sensor and for your sensor to recognize it.

Iso is a digital way to boost the light in an image. A high Iso makes photos grainy. A pro might look for an iso of 50-100, but 200-400 can also be really effective.

Photos have so much digital information and you can manipulate every pixel. You will see more digital noise in video faster if you boost it. In certain situations, you won't have a choice but to increase the iso, like in documentary settings.

"Sometimes getting that soundbite and having a video file is better than having nothing."

LESSON 3: B ROLL

Lesson 3 focuses on B-Roll, what it is, what it means, why it's important, why it's Sara's favorite thing. B-roll is alternate footage that can be interspersed in with the main footage.

"B Roll Is the act of filming footage that is going to aid your story. B Roll can be so beautiful and it can push stories to places that they may not have been able to go without that footage."

HOW TO TAKE GREAT B-ROLL

Step 1: Hold Steady
Hold your camera as steady as you can. Use your hands or use tools to stabilize your camera while you take your B-Roll.

Step 2: Count To Ten
Make sure in all the excitement and anxiety of filming that you get enough footage. That's why counting to ten is really helpful.

"Even if you don't have access to all the tools and all the tricks and the most exciting story, you can tell something so beautiful just from holding your shots."

SLOW MOTION

Filming in slow motion means filming at 60 or 120 frames per second. Your phone can film at this frame rate. If you're using a camera you will need to switch the frame rate.

B Roll Cheat Sheet
Get B Roll if you can.

- It' s better if the B-Roll is footage of what people are talking about.
- Use a wide variety of shots, get some wides, get some tights, get some mediums.
- If you can't film what the people are talking about, film something complimentary to it.

"My number one go-to is nature. When I'm struggling with a topic, I'll get it. Slow motion. I'll get really pretty angles. I'll use my cell phone, audio recorder to put it outside in the Bush with me and just get natural sound so that I can get some birds, some trees, some water, you bring all of those pieces together and you can tell some of the most beautiful stories."

LESSON 4: INTERVIEWS

Lesson 4 is about Interviews and Sara talks about how to set them up just by being creative with what you have. You will need at minimum one camera and one microphone.

Your camera could be:

- Your iphone
- Your Webcam
- An actual camera

If you have lighting, that's even better.

The next best option is two cameras, one microphone and lighting.

"Two cameras is just super, super ideal because it creates more freedom and flexibility when you're editing."

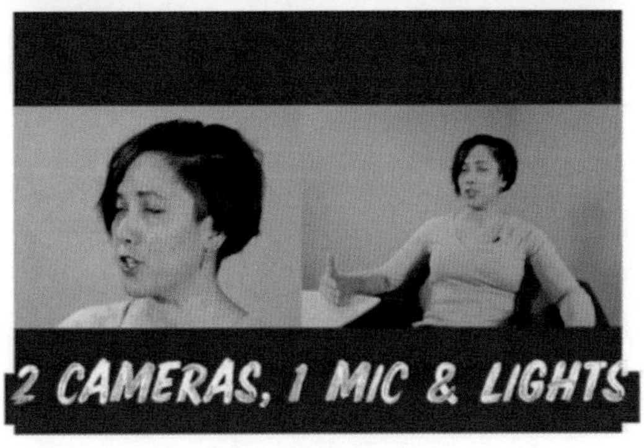

HOW TO SET UP A TWO CAMERA INTERVIEW

1. The first camera you're setting up is your main camera, your A cam. Take your main camera and you set it up as your main interview shot.
2. If you're doing something super corporate stick to a medium shot.
3. If you're doing a documentary or art or something beautiful, you get to frame it.
4. Your second camera can be a little bit more playful, a little bit tighter and more profile-like. Go ahead, get creative with this process.

"You know, we are being isolated, but we have this really cool thing of technology. And just because you are isolated, doesn't mean that you can't use the things in your house, the people in your house, the things in your backyard to get footage of that, you can also be reaching out to others that you can't access right now, physically via these creative ways."

In this lesson, Sara interviewed her mom and had her record herself on her Mac and also on her iphone to give more than one perspective. Even during this time of pandemic, you can connect with the people in your network and use the things in your space to make interesting film. Don't be afraid to ask for help!

"Reach out to someone you admire on Instagram or YouTube or whomever, maybe a cousin, an auntie, a friend, a teacher. If you don't have professional cameras, it doesn't matter. Your I-phones do these things. Your iPad will do these things. If you don't have them ask to borrow someone's and see what's possible."

LESSON 5: TRANSITIONS

Transitions can be fun and you can do them easily at home thanks to Boomerang, TikTok and Instagram. You're probably already using transitions without even thinking about it. They can even help you tell stories.

Transitions you might be familiar with:
You've probably seen the viral TikTok videos where someone snaps their fingers and changes outfits. What they're doing is using the exact same framing in each video and substituting the subject.

You can take something that's in the frame, throw out of the frame and have someone catch it again.

Another really popular one is making your camera go all the way black by blocking it completely and pulling it out. After the transition, the subject can be in a completely different setting.

Tips for playing with transitions:

- Make sure your frames line up when you're doing the actions.
- Be creative
- Don't let any of this advice limit you
- Go have fun with it

LESSON 6: MUSIC VIDEOS

Lesson 6 has Sara's tips to help you kind of get the best possible music videos that you can for yourself. One way to make a video is just to pick up your instrument and be playing right here in front of the camera. But what if you want to do something more intricate?

You could do a two-camera set up like we talked about in the interview video. Set up one camera on you with your guitar and the other camera can be the creative camera.

PULLING IT ALL TOGETHER:

"If you start recording both cameras at the same time and do a live session, you can keep your main camera on a tripod locked and set, and you can use your second camera to float and get creatives of the same moment. And then you could use the two shots together in post to create a beautiful, beautiful moment."

Sara shared two examples where she did this, once for her uncle's music video and once for her cousin singing live at an event. In both instances she used a locked off camera and a free moving camera to capture different moments.

Tip: If you're alone and don't have someone to record with a second camera, integrate B-roll instead.

AUDIO

Audio can be tricky. Ideally you want to use a microphone but if you're just filming art, try to keep the background as quiet as possible.

Be creative and see where creating a music video can take you!

LESSON 7: STOP MOTION

The premise behind stop motion is that you are moving the object yourself, but in editing, you're cutting out where you see the human interaction. If you have toys or action figures, you can make a whole film just by using stop motion in your house. If you can paint, you can animate things.

Stop Motion is:

- a really easy way to make titles and to make any story you want come to life
- a really fun way to animate things that otherwise wouldn't have had movement
- As a process, long, but it can be fun
- Therapeutic

Basically this is the process:

1. Write a story or a script.

2. Use Muppets, stock characters or household objects.

3. Move the characters or objects around.

4. Edit out you moving them.

Stop motion doesn't just have to be video, you can also do it in photos. What will you use to create your first stop motion video?

LESSON 8: TIPS AND TRICKS

This lesson is full of tips and tricks to help you make the best possible videos.

LIGHTING

Before you film, start by assessing the lighting:

- How is it in the space you're in?
- Would it be better if you were outside?
- Would it be better if you were in the shade outside?
- What kind of natural light can you get?

Tips:
Daylight is beautiful. Direct daylight can be harsh and aggressive with facial shadows.

Doorways can provide great lighting for video because of the way light bounces on the subject's faces.

Magic Hour is a great time to shoot

MAGIC HOUR: when the sun is horizontal and gives an opportunity for lens flares.

SMILES

Next up are tips about smiles.

> *"I love footage of smiles because I think it's contagious. I think that if I'm feeling good, you might feel that resonating on your side of the camera and I think that's so important."*

Connect with your subject and help them feel safe. One of Sara's tips is to, when groups are up close and squishy, get them to look at each other. They will laugh about being so close together and it helps you capture some great smiles in the moment.

SLOW MOTION WALK

Sara likes to walk with groups at weddings, encourage them to give a nod to the camera or a thumbs up and she films it all in slow motion which makes it look really cool.

Using all the tips and tricks in this series, you can get creative about making video in your home and with your loved ones. Make a music video, try to have fun on TikTok, interview your parents and tell the stories you've always wanted to tell. Enjoy yourself making cool videos and wash your hands!

TEACHING WITH CHRISTINE M'LOT

Since she was a child, Christine M'Lot knew when she grew up she wanted to be a teacher. From Swan Lake First Nation, but born and raised in Winnipeg, Manitoba, M'Lot says she was really lucky she always knew she wanted to work with children, and that school was something she always liked and helped her out a lot.

"I even used to make my little sister be my student and I would teach her things and give her homework, which probably really sucked for her, but it was fun for me," said M'Lot.

Of course she couldn't just head straight to the classroom, she had to learn how to teach. So she went to the University of Winnipeg for a five-year program, where she was part of an integrated program.

The integrated program meant not only was she learning what she wanted to teach, but they also have to pick a teachable major and a minor, so what subject areas they want to teach.

For M'Lot, she says what she really liked about her program was that they were in classrooms and for placements she was there to observe and get a feel of what kind of class she would like to teach. From there, she knew she wanted to be a high school teacher.

M'Lot teaches English for students in grades 9–11, as well as a grade 12 global issues course and a mandatory grade nine truth and reconciliation course, which she says students are shocked to learn about the history.

"Oftentimes, their middle years education kind of consists of all the nice things about Indigenous topics and they don't really get into the hard truth yet," said M'Lot.

She says she also tries to make aspects of the course positive, such as Indigenous contributions to society and teaches them aspects about her culture as well because students would be sad when leaving the classroom.

Even though she is teaching students and is doing what she loves, M'Lot faced many personal obstacles to get where she is today.

She went through a difficult time in high school, and started acting out and falling into a negative lifestyle of drugs and alcohol.

"Addiction runs in my family and so I always kind of grew up thinking like, 'Oh, I'm never going to be like that.'"

M'Lot was really close to not being able to graduate and become a teacher, until her boyfriend started getting her to think about her choices and what she really wanted in life.

"He noticed that I was doing all these stupid things and he's like, 'Why are you getting drunk every weekend? Why are you doing this? You want to be a teacher.' And he really helped me get on a good track," said M'Lot.

She said the questions he asked her and the things he said to her were really powerful and "exactly" what she needed in that moment.

Now, she tells youth who may encounter similar things she went through to stick to who you are and to always remember your goals, and says it was really important for her to be a teacher because she has always had that end goal and was something she knew she wanted to do.

"Stick to your goals and surround yourself with people who are doing the types of things that you want to do. Don't surround yourself with people who are going to be negative influences on you," said M'Lot.

And if there's one thing she can tell people, and she tells this to her students all the time, it would be: do things now that your future self will thank you for.

ONLINE PRESENCE FOR ARTISTS

Diana Hellson

View the videos in this series online! Scan the QR code, or visit http://www.tigurl.org/aop

Diana Hellson, also known as MAMARUDEGYAL MTHC and founder of Afro-Indigenous hiphop and entertainment group Rudegang Entertainment, spent years working on DIY projects and free software and wants to share how you can create digital media on a tight budget. She is a multi-disciplinary artist with a focus on hip hop, R & B, filmmaking, photography and graphic arts. Her lesson series is going to focus on her three favorite forms of digital media, which are photography, filmmaking, and graphic art.

This series by Diana Hellson is intended for artists who are new to the industry and who are really interested in learning how to find their footing and get grounded as new artists. Diana Hellson is also known as Mamarudegyal MTHC, the cofounder of Vancouver-based Rudegang Entertainment.

Diana's first tip is really simple: BE YOURSELF.

LESSON 1: BE AUTHENTIC WHEN BRAND BUILDING

"There are so many carbon copies of musicians who are already really famous and to be frank, we don't need anymore of them. We need new people. Explore the different parts of yourself in order to stand out from your peers, from other artists in your genre, in your scene, who are vying for the same opportunities as you."

"Tap into your true, authentic self and figure out what that means for you," Diana advises. That means asking yourself these questions:

What is your brand going to look like?

What is the aesthetic of your artistry?

Experiment and find what works for you. Think about the most unique part of yourself, even if it's something people tease you about. Diana encourages artists to enjoy the things they love and integrate those things into their brand.

"Just rock it. People are going to stand with you when you become unbothered about who you are and you build your brand and your brand identity off of genuine parts of who you are as an artist and as a person."

Eventually your career may evolve to a point where you have to worry about corporate interests but when you are first establishing your brand as an artist, you are in the drivers' seat and you don't have to worry what anyone else thinks from a contractual perspective.

"Enjoy your time as a free artist before having somebody come in and put their foot in your career and tell you what to say and do and wear or what not to say and do or wear. You have the opportunity now to completely express yourself."

How will you define your brand?

LESSON 2: YOUR BIO

Your social media pages need bios to help people get to know who you are. Your bio should contain key information to educate your audience.

It should have:

- Who you are
- Where you came from
- What year you started doing music
- What project are you working on right now?

"Our social media page pages, our artists' pages, is where we want industry professionals and new supporters who've never heard of us before to stumble upon us, discover us and learn about us and decide to stick around."

Larger things like grant applications, festival applications, showcase applications need different lengths of biographies. Diana likes to have her bio and all of her team member's bios handy in her notes section for grant applications. Here are some of her tips for bios:

- When applying on grants, make sure your bio is really easy to read and succinct.
- Keep adapting it
- Keep it updated

A current bio is so important. Diana says, "When you send it off to that next opportunity, you really want that person to have updated information about you and where you're at in your career and what's going on for you."

What will you include in your bio?

LESSON 3: BRAND IDENTITY AND CONSISTENCY

Diana says that being consistent with your brand identity can be easy to miss in the beginning but is more and more important as you grow in your career.

"Once you get to a point in your career where you're trying to enter the industry, you really want to have your brand identity so that you can have your brand assets completely consistent, that all share a general vibe, a general aesthetic or a color palette."

Brand assets should have a similar look and feel so people can see they go together. These assets include:

- cover photo
- profile picture
- Logo

What does consistency mean for the way people experience your brand?

"They saw your really good bio on the festival application. They're going to go to your Facebook page. They're going to be met with this beautiful layout, this beautiful profile picture, beautiful cover. They're going to take you seriously right away."

Keeping a consistent aesthetic through your music, fashion, photoshoots, brand assets makes a big difference.

> *"It is very important if you are stepping into the industry to make sure your branding and your aesthetic are really well identifiable. Our opportunities come from being noticed.The image of looking that professional will stay with you."*

What consistent feel do you want your brand to have?

LESSON 4: THE IMPORTANCE OF PROFESSIONAL LOOKING CONTENT

In this lesson we are going to talk about the value of creating a set of social media posters to promote yourself and establish your presence. You might use posters to promote your artist page, your latest album or a project you're working on.

That poster should include:

- album name
- release date
- where to find your album

Make sure your consistent aesthetic is present. If your album has a new aesthetic, make sure use those exact same colors within:

- your social media posters
- your icons

- your fonts
- Your album cover

Tip: Make sure the size of your poster is exactly what Facebook wants it to be.

Why is that sizing so important?

> *"Nothing is worse than designing a whole nice poster, making it nice and pretty, uploading it to Facebook, and then having Facebook crop it and losing all this other information over here. We don't want that to happen. And it's actually completely unnecessary."*

Make sure that the canvas of the poster you're designing is the exact size that you need it to be when you upload it.

Not sure what size you need? Google it. If you make it the wrong size at first, here's how to find out how to fix it:

Google "how to change the size of my canvas + whatever it is you are working in (photoshop, lucidpress, illustrator etc)"

Want to make sure your poster is even?

Photoshop and Lucidpress have smart grids to help you make sure everything is in alignment.

What will you promote with your first social media posters?

HOW TO CREATE A PORTABLE RECORDING BOOTH

Patrick Kelly

View the videos in this series online! Scan the QR code, or visit http://www.tigurl.org/booth

Hope is a professional Hip-Hop artist and performer from Leq'a:mel First Nation British Columbia. Inspired by Tradition, Hope uses the art of storytelling and rhyme to depict life on the reservation and illustrate to others what it is to be indigenous.

"As a beginner and non-engineer, it can be difficult to know where to start or what we really need in order to record our music. I hope these stories and tips can be useful to artists who would like to start building their own DIY booth."

In this video series, Patrick Kelly, co-founder of Rudegang Entertainment, shares how he created his recording booth and some tips and tricks he learned along the way. Based in Vancouver, Patrick is a hip hop artist who performs under the name Hope and is also part of the Indigenous rap duo Status Crew with his rhyme partner Doobie.

"Since I began making hip hop in 2010, I've had the opportunity to record music in a variety of booths from high-end to homie's closet."

"When I started thinking about how much money I would need to invest in the longterm to record my music, I realized that it was in my best interest to make a long-term investment so that I could have more freedom in the recording process. While this decision came with a number of obstacles and learning curves, it was ultimately the best choice for someone in my circumstances. I decided to meet every obstacle and learning curve with an action to help me to continue progressing to a point where my recordings didn't have to sound like home studio recordings anymore."

HOME STUDIO SETUP OPTIONS:

Closet setups can be problematic for sound quality.

Mattress booths need 2-4 mattresses, can be cumbersome, costly and potentially unsanitary.

Another option is the reflection filter, which is affordable and works well but isn't ideal for all-around sound-proofing.

When you're looking for a home recording booth that is portable, you're going to want to keep these characteristics in mind:

- Effective soundproofing
- Easy set up and takedown
- Compact for storage and travel
- Doesn't take up too much room

These factors are what makes the Blanket-Style recording booth Patrick's ideal choice.

"Typically a blanket style recording booth is put together with a series of PVC piping and sound blankets surrounding the microphone setup. This allows the user to dismantle and pack the studio and also transport the booth with relative ease."

The Rudegang Recording booth features:

- Two sound blankets with grommets hanging across their gigantic window
- One sound panel on the wall
- Two hanging panels made of a dissected rug with soundproofing foam sewn on
- A toy net hanging above the booth filled with extra foam
- Soundproof foam lining the corner
- Another rug on the floor
- A divider panel behind the microphone
- Four blackout curtains

"Closing off the space with this setup, we're able to achieve the type of silence we would pay hundreds of dollars for in a high-end studio, but I didn't get my booth this way overnight."

Patrick's journey to the ideal soundbooth was lined with challenges.

- buying the wrong gear
- ineffective setups
- crashed recording sessions
- Research
- info interviews with real engineers

While these homemade studios aren't as high quality as a professional recording studio, they are affordable, accessible and safe during this time of quarantine. What will you record in your DIY recording booth?

LESSON 2: GEAR: THE RUN DOWN

This lesson focuses on the very basics of recording gear so you can get a sense of what you might need to record your music and why. Rudegang Entertainment came up with its current gear through trial and error over the years.

> *"It's important to make sure that we are recording the best quality sound possible on our end to make sure that our friends who mix and master our music have the best opportunity possible to make our songs sound great."*

Rudegang uses:

- Shure microphone
- Kaotica Eyeball (which includes a pop filter and features additional soundproofing)
- Rycote Shockmount
- Good Mic Stand
- 2 pairs of headphones (one for the artist and one for the recording engineer)
- M-Box Mixer (simple two channel)

Gear can be expensive but there are ways to save money.

MONEY SAVING TIPS

Search Kijiji or FB Marketplace for gently used gear or borrow from people who own equipment you need.

If you can't find gear used on the cheap, these are some tips to get the best gear at the best price:

- Save up
- Finance
- Shop at your local music store
- Do your research

Doing your research looks like:

- Asking local music store staff who can be a great resource
- researching product competitors
- Reading customer reviews
- Talking to music professionals in your community
- Watching YouTube videos that test the product

Where will you start your hunt for gear?

LESSON 3: BARE BASICS OF RECORDING GEAR

This lesson focuses on the very basics of recording gear so you can learn what you might need to record your music and why.

MICROPHONES

"While I am certainly no expert on the technology or science behind microphones, experience has taught me that quality absolutely makes a difference.There is absolutely no shame in whatever quality of mic you choose to record with.

But if you're going to go through the fuss of building yourself a great booth with sound quality in mind, I highly recommend investing in a top quality microphone to record with if all goes well, your investment will eventually be able to pay for itself."

The shockmount and microphone stand are pieces of equipment that can be easy to overlook but may be really important depending on the type of microphone you have.

One of Patrick's early missteps was overloading the weight limits of the shockmount. That meant more foreign sound was getting into the recordings because the new mic was too heavy for the shockmount. A loose mic stand also had to be replaced to dial in on clearer sound.

To recap: Get the best quality microphone you can on donation, trade or finance and pay attention to the details because they can significantly impact your recording quality.

"Things like foam, a pop filter, shockmount, and a good sturdy mic stand can make the difference between a good clean recording or a muddled recording."

LESSON 4: SOFTWARE AND LEARNING THE ROPES

This lesson focuses on software and music recording options.

DAWS, or Digital Audio Workstations are a type of audio recording software that lets you connect to and interact with mixers and instruments to create a professional recording. There are plenty of choices depending on your budget, recording needs and experience. Because software will have key differences between them, research is really important.

You might want to start with Reaper or Audacity, which are free to get yourself started before you invest in an expensive DAW.

That said, if you are looking to do something more serious, you're going to want more serious equipment. Some trusted names include Logic, ProTools, Reason or Ableton Live.

Rudegang Studios uses ProTools as their DAW.

DAWs might look confusing in the beginning, but you can learn how to use them through online tutorials. Patrick did information interviews with engineers in his community to learn more.

Local workshops are another way to learn about DAWs.

Don't be afraid to ask for help! There are lots of people out there who love supporting new artists on the rise.

To recap:

1. There are lots of options for DAWS, you will find one that works for you.

2. Do your research before you buy.

3. Use free DAWs to practice.

4. Check out free online tutorials

5. Ask for help locally from people who know what they're talking about

With all this knowledge base to build your home studio, you have a lot of opportunities to pursue to start making music.

TIKTOK WITH THELAND KICKNOSWAY

Theland Kicknosway may be young, but is already proving to be someone to keep an eye on in the future.

Kicknosway is Cree and Potawatami from Walpole Island First Nation in Ontario, but currently lives in Ottawa, ON.

He is 17-years-old and currently still in high school, but has plans for what he wants to do when it comes to his post-secondary education.

"Some of the things that actually interest me are the Indigenous Education Course, but in general, I think education is important, not only western, more what they teach you in school, but also indigenous education as well," said Kicknosway.

"So to mix both of those worlds together, I think is really awesome. So I'm really looking down that pathway."

Even though he hasn't yet made the transition from high school to university, he still has advice to give himself when he eventually does, and it's to know that whatever it is he is doing it's a good thing.

"It's for not only my own learning and my own education, but also for this opportunity to learn as much as I can now. So then I can teach others some of the stuff that I was able to learn at post-secondary," said Kicknosway.

He also says going into it, he knows that his ancestors will be there to guide him through the western and societal way of education while still maintaining traditional ways.

"So I can hold both of those types of learning and then moving forward, learning about how to teach others and inspire others at the same time," said Kicknosway.

In terms of inspiring others, Kickosway is already doing that. He was the recipient of the Culture, Heritage, and Spirituality award from Indspire, and is the youngest person to receive it.

Kicknosway says he is very honoured to hold the title, and everyone on the team that put the awards together to help make people's lives better is "so amazing."

"The Indspire awards, that was an amazing time. And when I was receiving my award, we were in Winnipeg and it was really great to meet all of the recipients, all the laureates and just that was an amazing time and I hope everyone can feel how I felt during those couple of days."

Even though Kicknosway has achieved a lot in such little time, he has also run into obstacles with the loss of his childhood friend being a huge one.

"That was very hard for me, because at that time I was making the transition from middle school to high school. And there is a big learning curve there, because the homework gets tougher... and so for me, it was a lot for myself to take in at that point," said Kicknosway.

He said to overcome that obstacle he had to acknowledge his friends life and to be thankful for the time he had with him, which he still does today and will do "forever."

"He has definitely taught me a whole lot about how we need to appreciate life. And so everything I do is just to honour him."

Theland has also become a leader in using TikTok to share his dance moves, culture and advocacy with the world, attracting over 380,000 followers and 9 million likes to his creative video content!

WORKING WITH EPOXY RESIN TO CREATE JEWELLERY

Kyrstin Dumont

View the videos in this series online! Scan the QR code, or visit http://www.tigurl.org/epoxy

Kyrstin Dumont is a 19 year old Algonquin First Nations Anishinaabe kwe who has dedicated her life to the Indigenous community through her advocacy and activism work with organizations such as UNICEF Canada, the Child Welfare League, OCDSB and C.A.S. where she is able to shed light and awareness on issues that affect herself and her community. Kyrstin manages to find time to model and work with Indigenous designers and artists as well as continuously furthering her knowledge in traditional Indigenous art forms.

LESSON 1: THE DO'S AND DON'TS OF RESIN

When you're dealing with resin, you're going to want:

a silicone mat - to protect your surface

Disposable gloves - or it'll make your hands very, very hard and uncomfortable, just like cement

Finger gloves can replace disposable gloves - but be careful your palms don't touch the resin

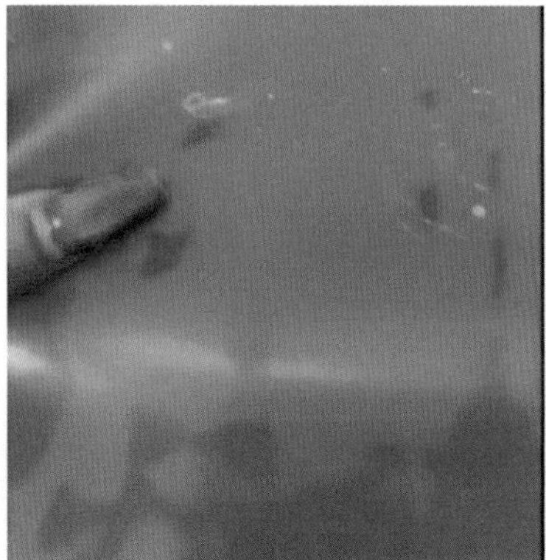

Plastic tools - instead of items you find in your everyday kitchen

Fresh, clean and unused silicone molds so you don't get glitter, gold or other things stuck in your resin.

Plastic measuring cups. If you use glass or ceramic, it'll be very hard to clean.

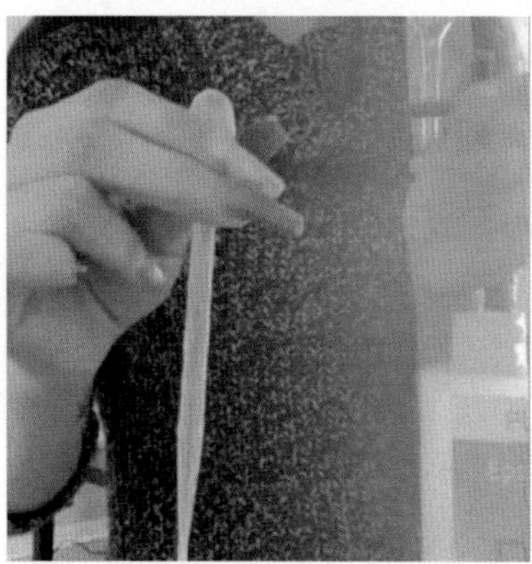

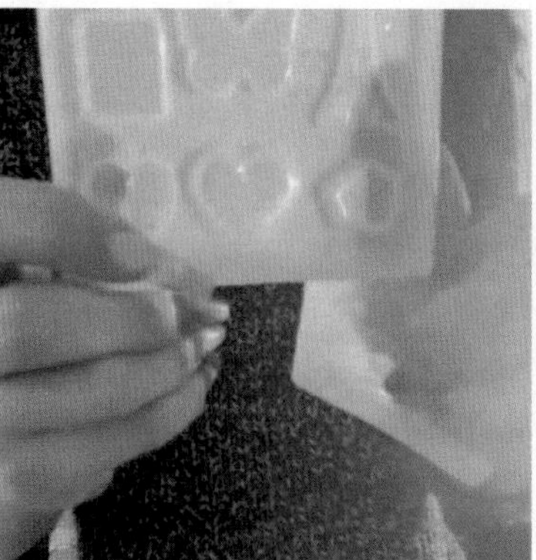

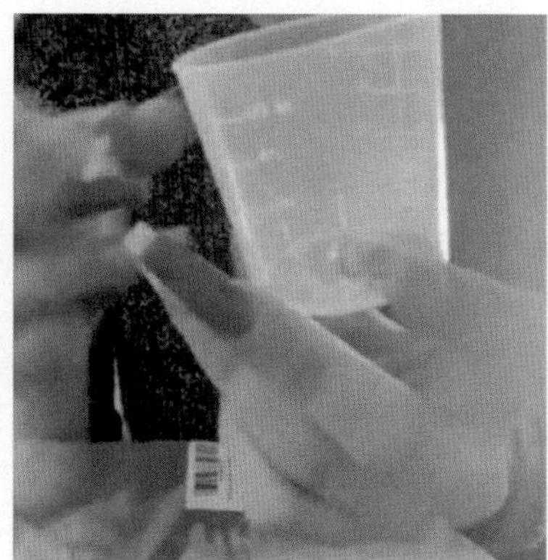

LESSON 2: HOW TO CREATE RESIN JEWELLERY

This lesson will show you how to create resin jewelry.

First, grab a large bow and turn on your tap. Wait until the water gets as hot as possible. Fill the bowl with hot water. Next, place the epoxy resin and the hardener in the hot water so it can liquefy.

Measure equal amounts of epoxy resin and hardener. If they aren't the same, curing will take longer.

Combine the two ingredients in a larger container. Use a small plastic spoon to help the epoxy out of its container if necessary.

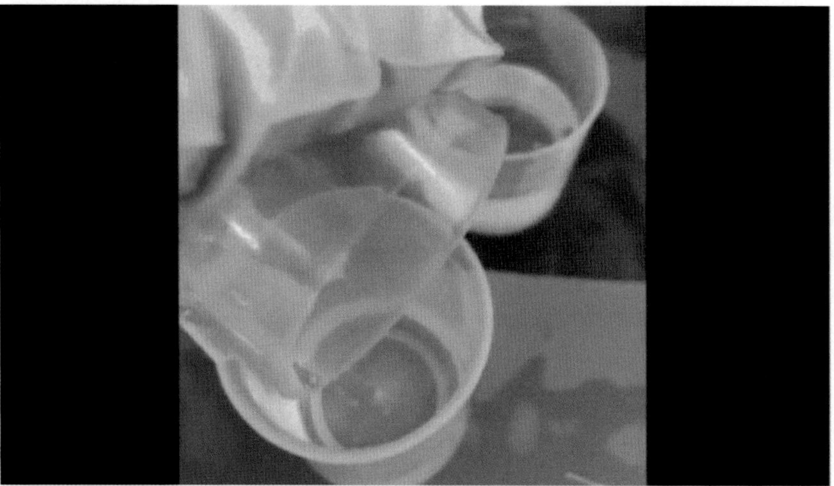

Mix them together with a small plastic spoon until there are no bubbles in the mixture.

HOW TO GET YOUR MOLDS READY

There are two ways to get your molds ready. One way is that you put the ingredients such as medicines or gold flakes in the molds before your mixture. Use this tool that looks like a small turkey baster to insert your mixture into the mold.

Kyrstin uses another technique which is to fill the molds and then adding the dried flower medicines carefully on top. She finds it an easier way to work with detailed jewelry pieces.

Kyrstin uses non-toxic epoxy as it makes her feel safer. She buys it off of Amazon.

The mixture takes 8 hours to cure. Once the pieces are cured, you should be able to remove them from the mold.

When cured, they should look crystal clear.

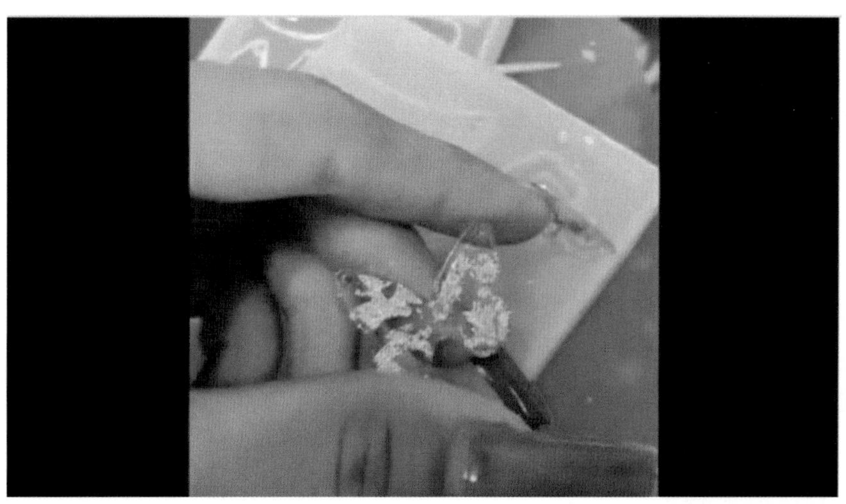

LESSON 3:

Kyrstin noticed that the resin was harder on one side and decided to file it down to even it out. She uses different shaped files to work on different pieces to get different results.

Tip: Your hands might get a little white, but don't be concerned as it's just the dust from the resin.

Kyrstin uses a rectangle file to smooth out any ridges and make it shine.

If you want your piece to be shinier, you can sand it down some more with sandpaper. It also helps remove white marks.

Wipe your resin piece down with a cloth to remove any excess powder that may be stuck on there.

It will look even better when it's all cleaned up!

LESSON 4: RESIN CHAIN WORK

First, you will need a tiny handheld drill like this:

JUMP RING:

a ring made of a bar or wire with plane ends abutted against each other, but not welded. (source: wordnik)

BAIL:

A finding that connects a pendant to a necklace. (source: Beadage)

Start drilling a hole in the top of the pendant in the middle.

Kyrstin likes to use E6000 glue to keep her bale strong and in place inside of the pendant.

She puts the glue on top of the bag so she can dip the bail inside and then put it directly in the pendant itself.

Like this:

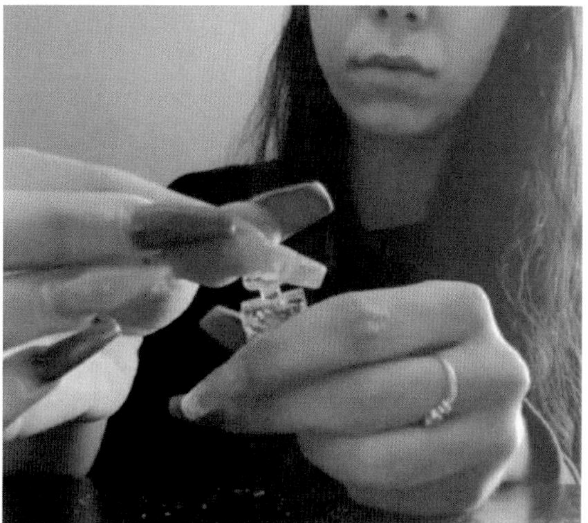

Your jumpring will be closed and circular, so you'll need to open it up so that it can go inside of the bail itself.

Once your jump ring is inside of the bail, you're going to want to close it a little bit so that it doesn't fall out while you grab the chain.

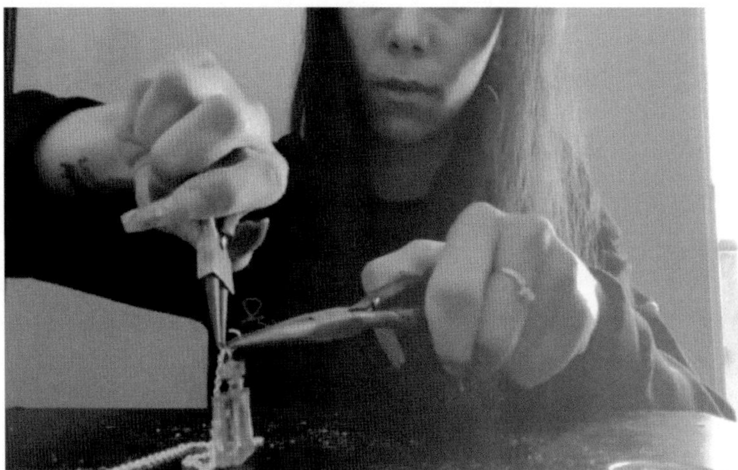

Once your chain is inside the jumpring, you need to secure it by closing the jumpring so the chain doesn't fall out.

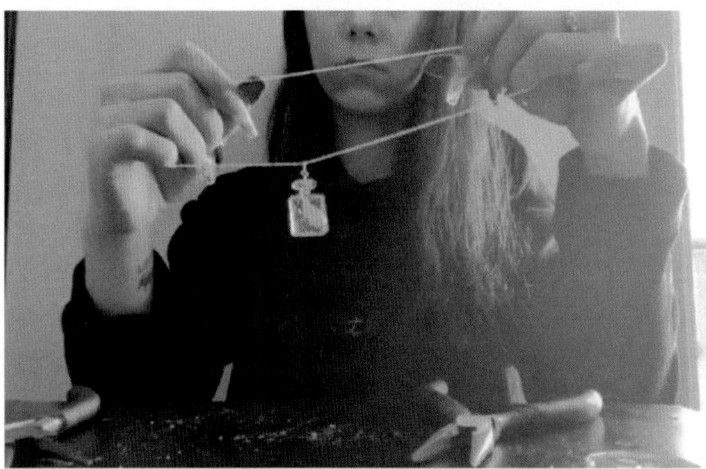

You have now created your first resin necklace! Congratulations!

PILOTING WITH RAVEN BEARDY

When Raven Beardy was growing up, she knew she wanted to get her pilot's license — she just didn't know she would make it into a career.

Beardy is originally from Shamattawa in northern Manitoba, but has also lived up in the north in places such as Pond Inlet, Grise Fiord, and Cambridge Bay.

"Growing up in isolation up in Shamattawa where the only way to get things in and out was by plane," said Beardy.

"So I saw that as a little kid and I actually also got my medevac child as well. I just thought it was really cool, planes were really cool to me."

Beardy remembers a time when she was seven the power went out in her community and they had to call the medevac to come in.

"The community got together and actually lined up their snowmobiles along the runways so the plane could land. And I just really thought that was inspiring that the community got together," said Beardy.

But of course Beardy hasn't always been a pilot. She went to a three-year aviation program in southern Ontario that focused on Indigenous students to become what she is.

Beardy says one of the best things about her program was she wasn't the only one there that wasn't from far away and that everyone was "in the same boat."

She says there are many ways to go about getting a pilot's license and people just need to figure out what they want to do.

But of course, becoming the pilot she is today didn't come without its obstacles.

After flight school, Beardy says once someone is finished they usually start working for a flight company and start off on the ground doing jobs such as dispatcher or a customer representative to get a feel of the company.

"That's usually how it works. And when I graduated with many other pilots, like I was waiting on ground for five years before, or sorry, four years before I actually got a flight position. So it took a long time to get there," said Beardy.

She said it was discouraging at times and in the end she just powered through it, saying it's very rewarding in the end.

And if there were anything she could tell her younger self, it would be that just because she's Indigenous and a female it doesn't mean there would never be issues.

"If anything, it was more of an obstacle. I felt like, I had to prove myself even more and work harder than, the next person, which is not a bad thing," said Beardy.

"You're told that you're being Indigenous... [It will be] no problem finding a job or anything like that, but it's not true at all."

Beardy has achieved a lot of her goals, and says the hardworking people in her life such as her grandparents and seeing their work ethic helped her, along with her parents.

"I'm very fortunate to have a really great role models in my life."

PODCASTING

Jade Roberts

View the videos in this series online! Scan the QR code, or visit http://www.tigurl.org/podcasting

Jade Roberts, who is Woodland Cree from Lac La Ronge Indian Band in Northern Saskatchewan, produced this series to help you learn how to podcast. Jade currently lives in Saskatoon on Treaty Six territory. She is an educator and an artist who started podcasting two years ago. Jade is the creator and host of Still Here Still Healing. It started out as a show to bring awareness to the impacts of residential schools and also to talk to residential school survivors, to provide a platform for them to share their stories. She's sharing her lessons in podcasting with us so we can all learn.

LESSON 1: INTRO

"I believe that podcasting is a great way, a great form of storytelling. We have so many stories to share as Indigenous people, and this is just an awesome platform to get it across."

Over the course of the video series, Jade is going to teach how to set up an audio recording using an iPad. This is not normally the technique she uses to do her podcast, but she does use GarageBand which is available on Mac, iPhones and iPads.

LESSON 2: GARAGEBAND FOR IPAD SETUP

This lesson teaches how to set up Garageband on your ipad. The first thing you will want to do is open the app and select "Create a Song".

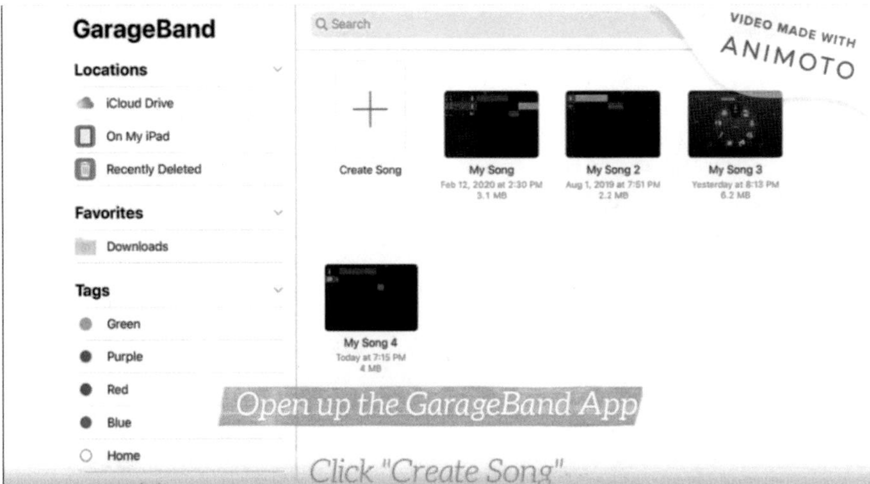

From there, this screen will appear:

If you scroll through there will be a bunch of different instrument options, like this one:

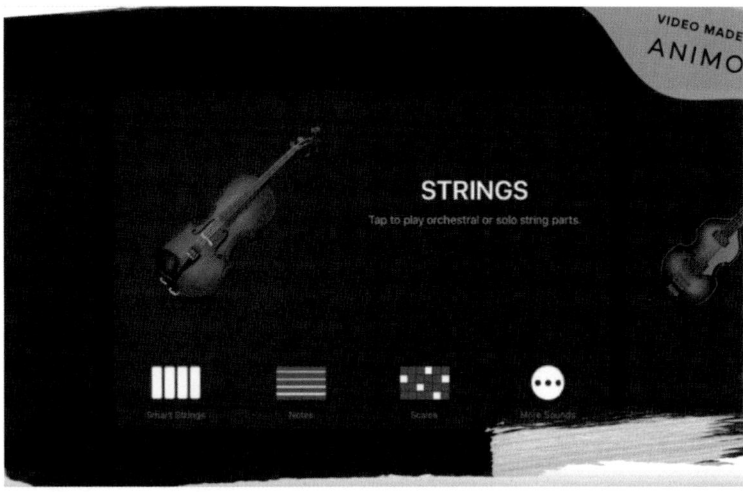

For this exercise, we will only be using the audio recorder. Select Voice in the bottom left to get started.

This is the screen that will come up next:

These controls are set to what they need to be set at so you don't need to really play around with them unless you really want to. On the left side, the green indicator going up and down indicates the mic is picking up your voice levels. This is a good thing.

You will see Fun and Studio on the top.

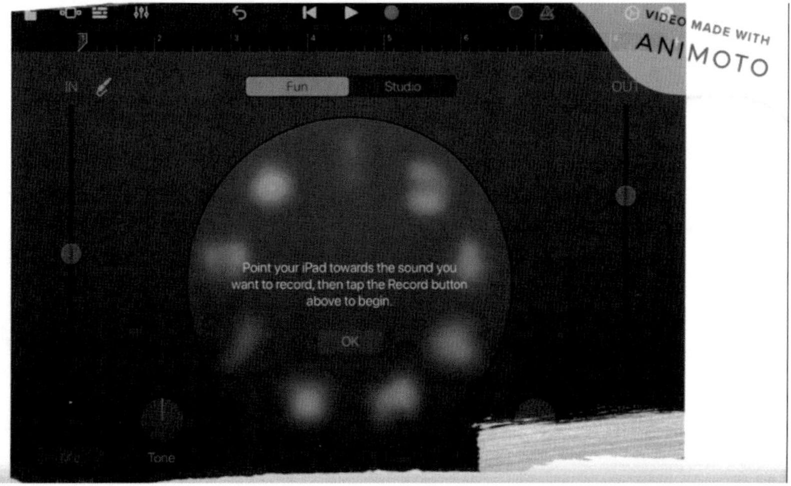

If you switch it to Fun you are going to get a bunch of different effects.

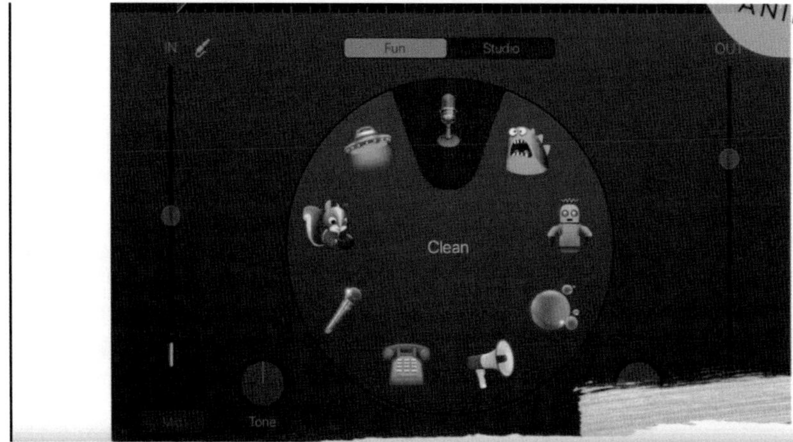

Using these effects you can change your voice and have a lot of fun. This feature is great for kids but it's not what we're going to be using today.

Back in studio view, click on the blue triangular metronome icon at the top. If you leave that on you will hear ticking in the background of your recording.

The icon on the top left that has squares and rectangles will take you to a new screen where you can see your recording.

This is where we will start from in the next lesson.

LESSON 3: GARAGE BAND RECORDING ON IPAD AND APPLE LOOPS

In this lesson, we're going to be looking at a GarageBand recording on iPad and we're also going to be looking at how to add Apple Loops. This is the screen we left off with in the second lesson and this is going to be our main workspace where we'll be doing our editing and adding our Apple Loops.

The microphone on the left hand side is going to be the layer for the vocals. You can use the plus sign in the bottom left to add additional vocals and instruments if you like. You might use two microphones if you have two people you are recording on different layers.

Since we are only working with one vocal track we can just delete the second microphone.

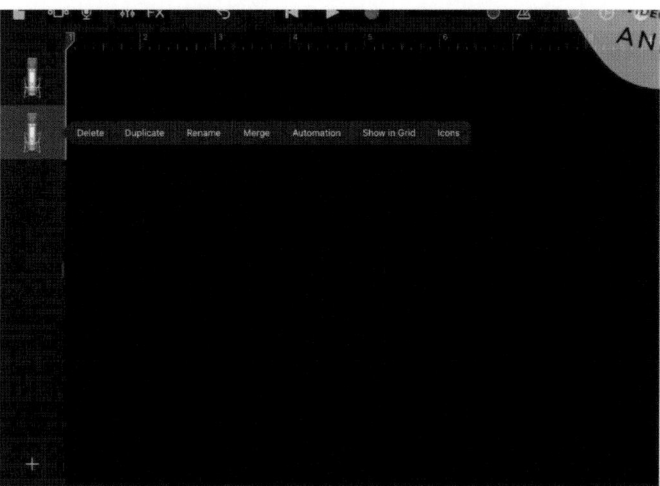

To record, click the red button and it will count down to start the recording.

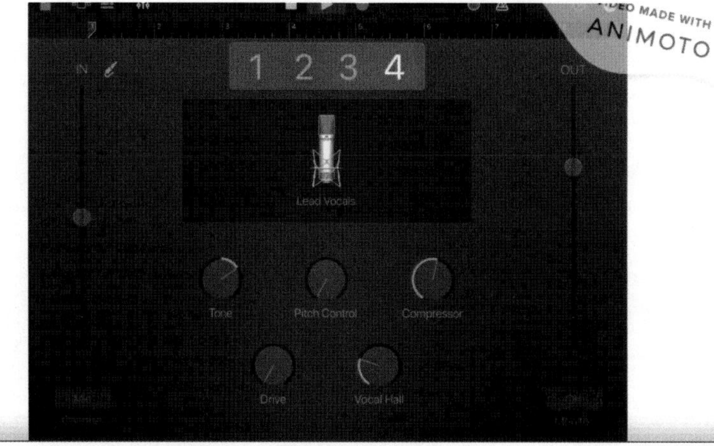

Hit stop when you are done and then you can preview the recording.

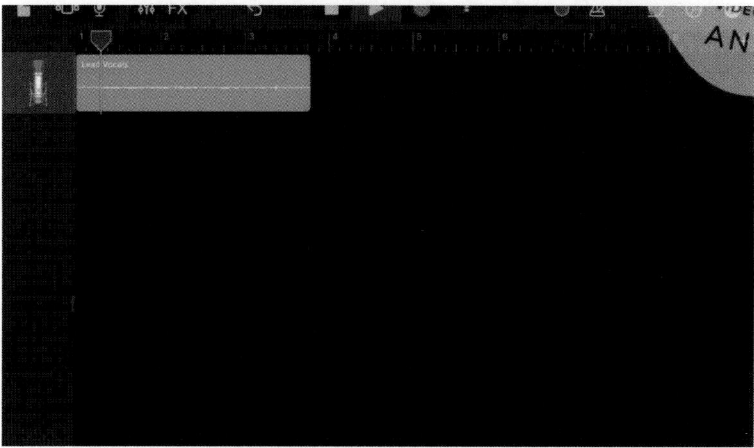

To edit out a section you aren't happy with, simply move the playhead to highlight the section you want to remove, hit "split" and "delete" to remove it.

If you want to add an intro before your vocal audio, you can drag your vocal segment over to make room for the music.

Next, go to the loop icon in the top right corner to get this menu for Apple Loops:

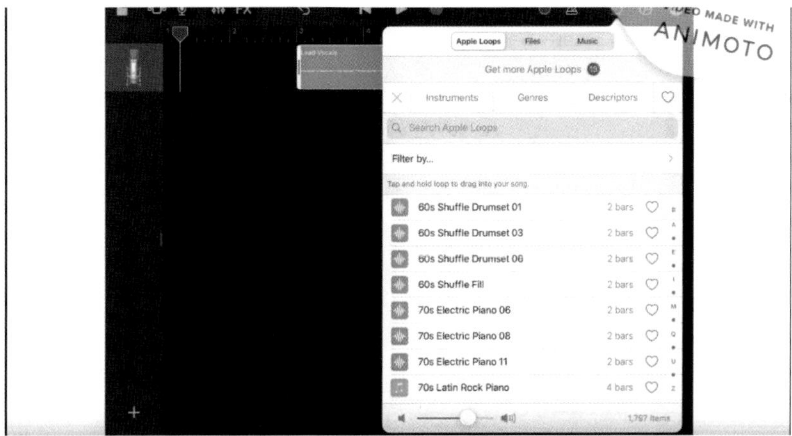

There are lots of free loops available, you can preview them before you drop them in to your recording. Clicking the heart next to a loop title will set it as a favourite, like this:

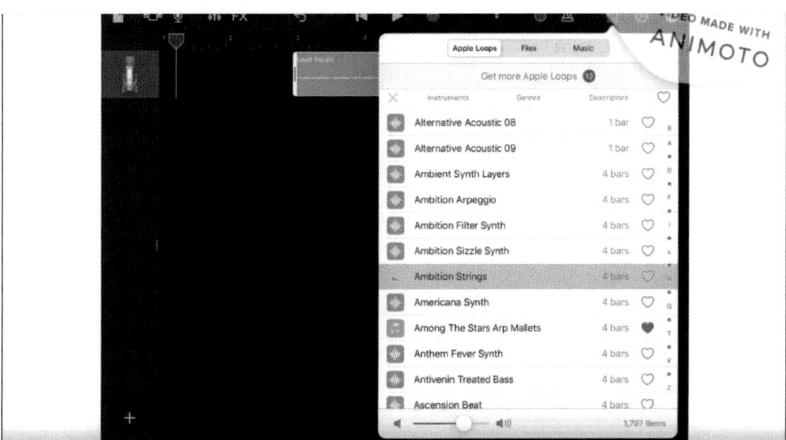

When you pick a loop you want to use, drag it over to your workspace:

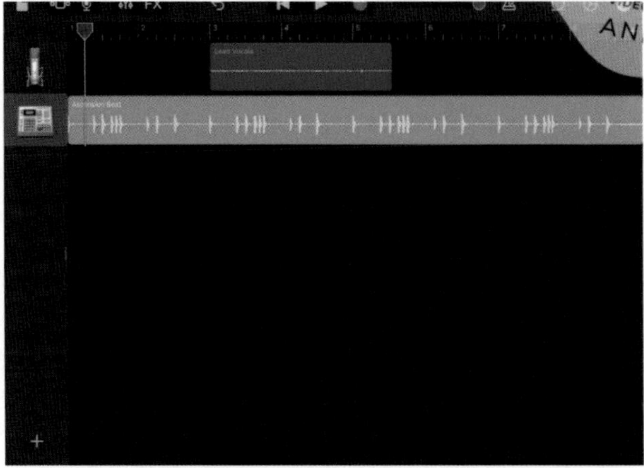

It will create a new layer. You can drag the far right hand side of the loop over to shorten it like this:

To close the gap between the loop and the vocals, you can just drag the vocals over like this:

To add more music after the vocals, you can drag a new loop over to the workspace to create a new layer like this:

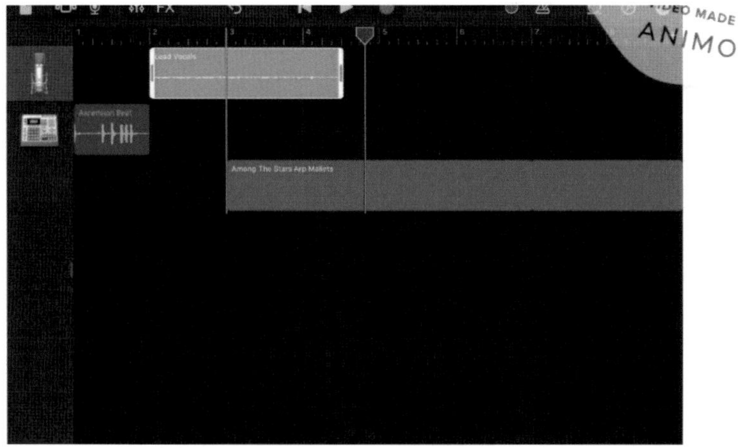

You can trim the loop and move it around just like we did with the other loop:

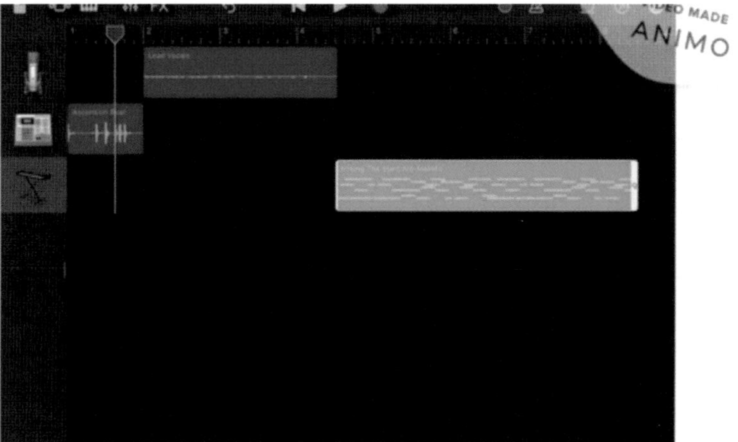

To add more vocals, line up the playhead with where you want the audio to start recording to ensure you aren't talking over the beat. Make sure the right layer is highlighted and hit record:

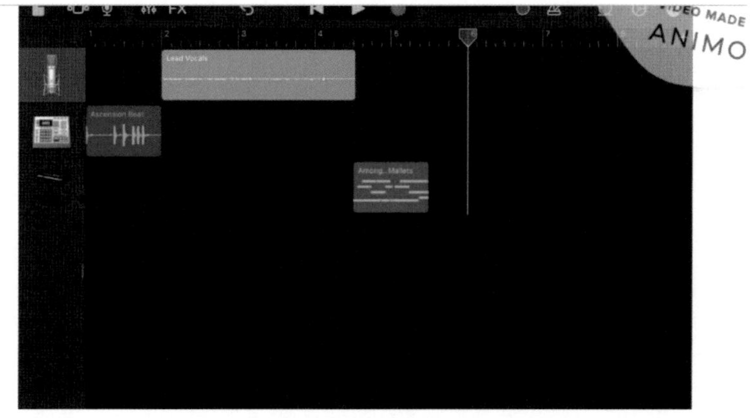

You will be counted back in to record more vocals and you can hit stop when you're done.

You can realign the vocals so they play after the beats if needed just by dragging the vocals section to the desired spot like this:

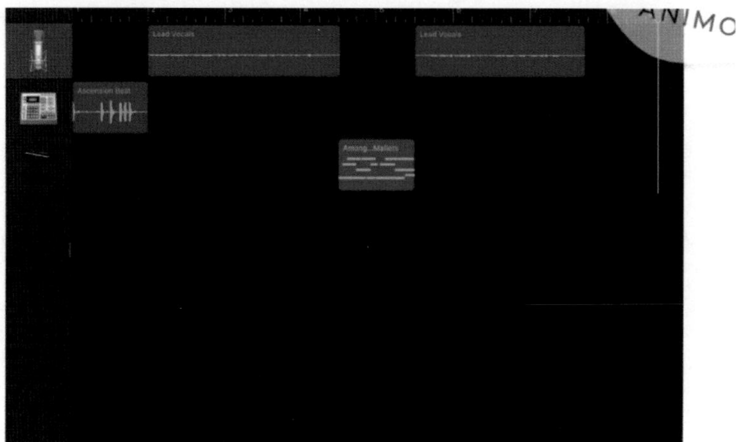

Drag the playhead back to the beginning to preview the whole recording.

GarageBand for iPad is in sections because the screen is so small:

You'll need to add more sections:

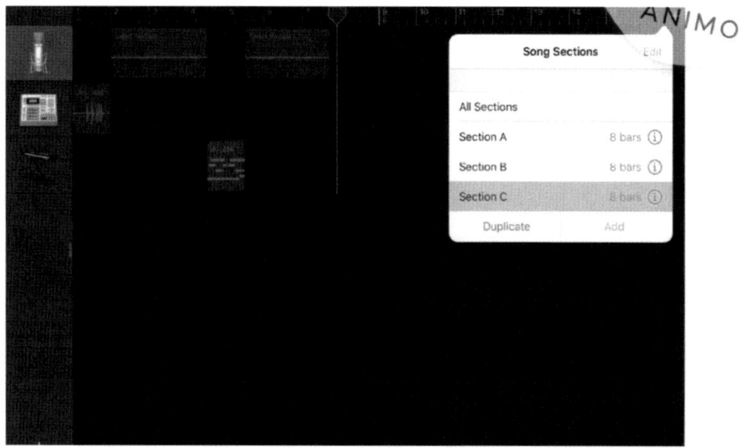

GarageBand for desktop doesn't use sections, but the iPad version does.

Under settings, you can set your audio to fade out:

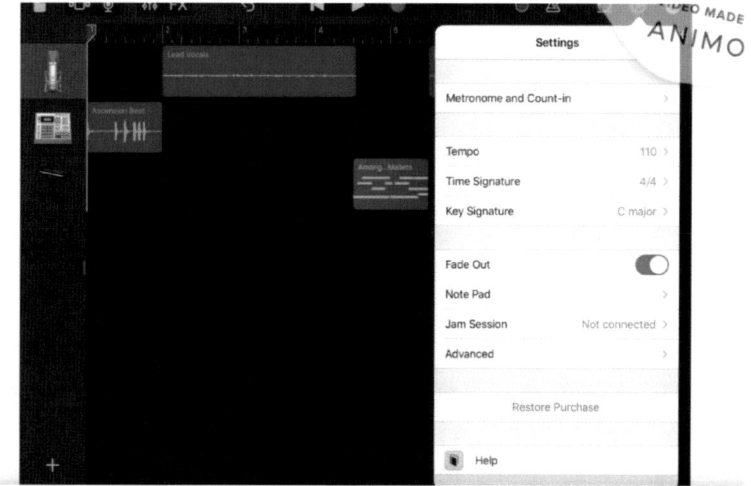

When you're done, if you go back to the main page, all of your recordings are stored in one place.

You don't have to worry about your recordings getting lost because GarageBand for iPad autosaves and stores on iCloud.

LESSON 4: EXTRAS - MORE ABOUT EQUIPMENT AND SHARING YOUR POD

This lesson talks about equipment and tips on how to share your podcast or your audio recordings.

GarageBand for iPad is so helpful if you want to record and don't have access to a computer. Jade first started recording on a ShureMV5, which is a USB condenser mic. It's advantages are that it's great for in person recording with one person and it's affordable. It's not as good for more than one person or if you're recording phone calls.

Jade's next setup was a Zoom H4NPro. Jade found this one had a learning curve but she could use it as a handheld or you can plug in a mic. She used an AudioTechnica mic with a cord and a mic stand. It's not a USB microphone so it has to be plugged into the Zoom to use it. The sound quality was good and you don't have to take your laptop with you to record. It's very portable

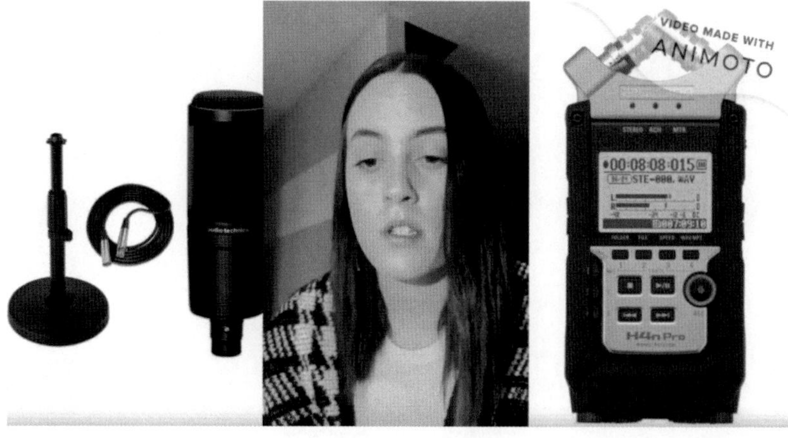

Jade's current setup looks like this:

Jade uses the Rodecaster Pro which is perfect for podcasting and you can plug in up to four microphones. You can also plug it into your laptop to record things like Zoom calls or your cellphone to record your phone calls. It also has a soundboard. She is still using the Audio Technica mic.

This is a Desktop view of GarageBand. When you're done recording, click Share to get this menu:

When you select "Share to iTunes", populate the fields in the popup box and click "Share".

Your recording will end up on iTunes as an m4A file.

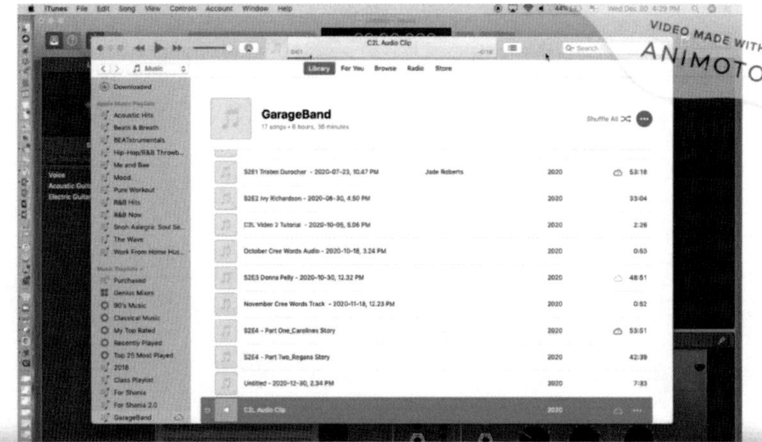

You're going to want to hit "File" and "Convert" and "Create MP3 Version":

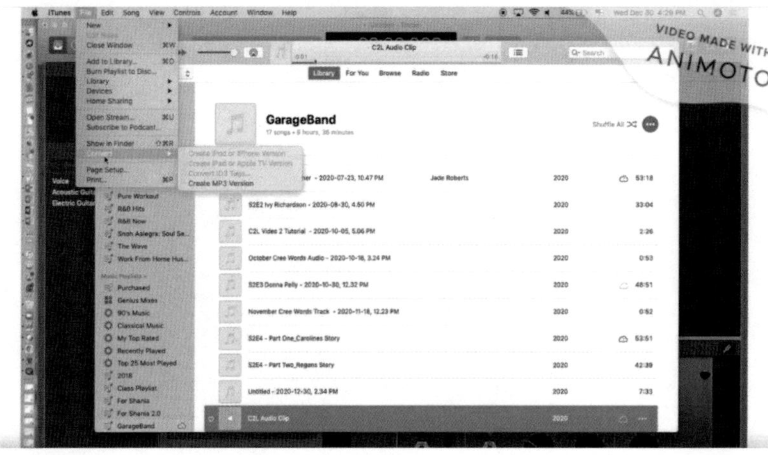

This is an important step if you want to upload your recording to your own website, PodBean or Anchor. When you do that conversion, you will have an M4A and an MP3 version in your library.

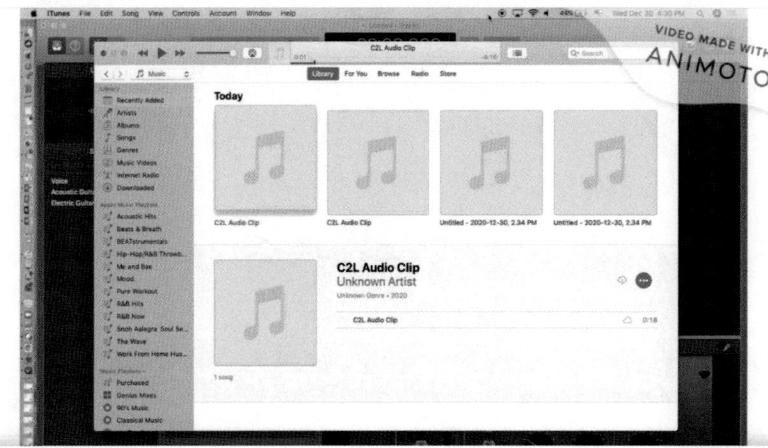

Wondering how to share your podcast onto things like Apple, Spotify, or Google? You must have an RSS feed and to get one of those, you have to put your show onto a hosting platform. Some of those can cost money but some are free. Currently Jade uses Podbean but is planning to switch to Anchor, which is free. Make sure to tune into Jade's podcast, "Still Here Still Healing" and give her a follow on Instagram!

HOW TO MAKE BANNOCK

Gabrielle Fayant

View the videos in this series online! Scan the QR code, or visit http://www.tigurl.org/bannock

Gabrielle Fayant is a Michif woman residing on traditional Algonquin territory. Gabrielle is one of the cofounders and co-CEO of an Indigenous youth-led organization called Assembly of Seven Generations. Gabrielle is called an auntie by many youth for sharing her knowledge so young people can make the best informed decisions for their well-being.

"As Indigenous people, we take care of our communities, we take care of each other and sometimes that means like we divide up what we have left."

Bannock is a food that can get you through quite a long period of time with very minimal ingredients. There are lots of different ways to make it, from frying it like frybread, adding toppings to make Indian Tacos, adding berries to the dough or serving it with Saskatoon Berry jam. It's a survival food and it's meant to be shared.

"Flour was always around. So let's make bread. You can make a lot with just a little bit. That's the cool thing about bannock."

This is a recipe that has been passed down for generations, from Nokomis (grandmother) to now and generations before that. While it's not the healthiest option for a lot people due to the gluten and carb content, it's traditional and with every pot of soup or chili there's usually bannock.

Here's what you'll need to get started:

- Flour (all purpose is fine.)
- Baking powder. Magic Baking Powder is the recommended brand thought it isn't what was used in this tutorial.
- Salt is optional, and is not for everyone.
- A bowl for mixing:
- A measuring cup and tablespoon are also helpful.
- A pan. You can pre-grease it.
- A cup of lukewarm water:

"Bannock is super easy to make. Once you have flour and baking soda, you can make so many different things. It's a foundation to do more baking and getting creative with baking too. It's trial and error, so don't be scared if your first batch doesn't turn out a hundred percent the way you wanted, just keep trying."

First, add flour by the cup. Behzig, in Anishinaabe, means one.

Niish means two.

Nswi means three.

Similarly, measure out three scoops of baking powder.

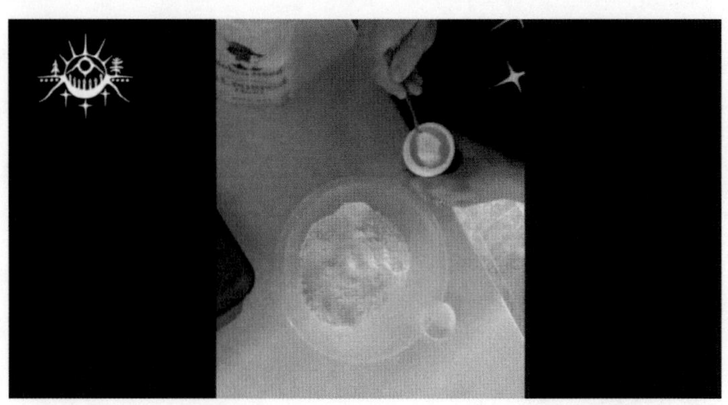

Add a pinch of salt (optional).

Mix all the ingredients together:

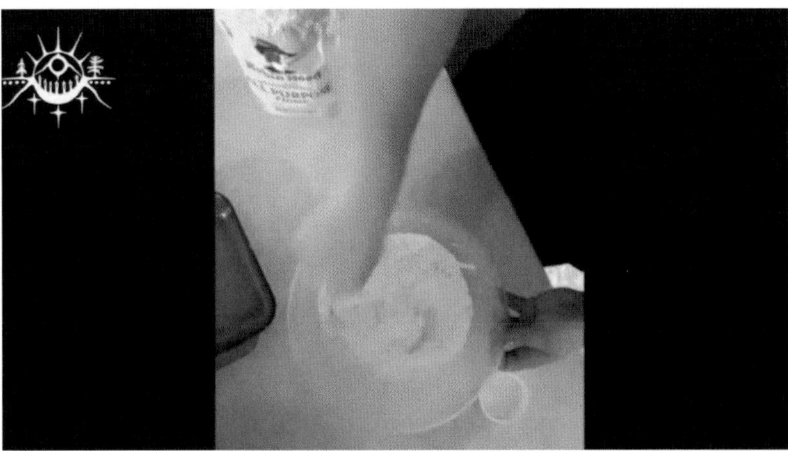

Mixing technique is important. Start off with a well, a hole in the middle of your bannock, like this:

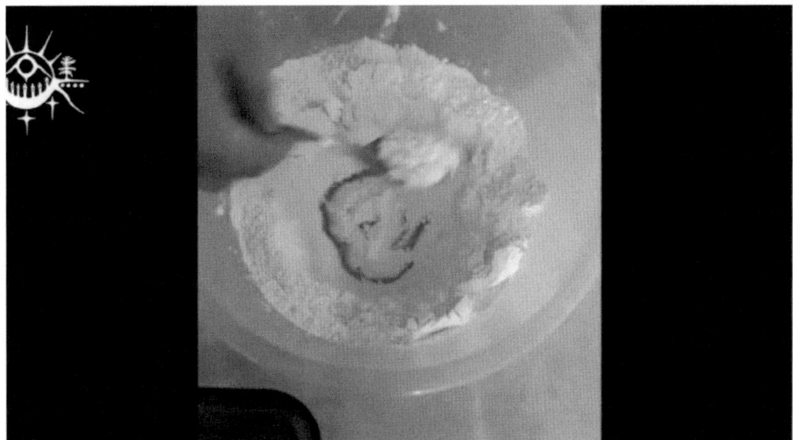

"You have to treat it like you would treat your partner. You've got to be gentle. You've got to be patient. You have to be thoughtful. If you take that time and you use ingredients properly and go at a slower pace, it's going to turn out really fluffy and tasty."

You have to eye out how much water to add. Start by filling up the well in your ingredients with water.

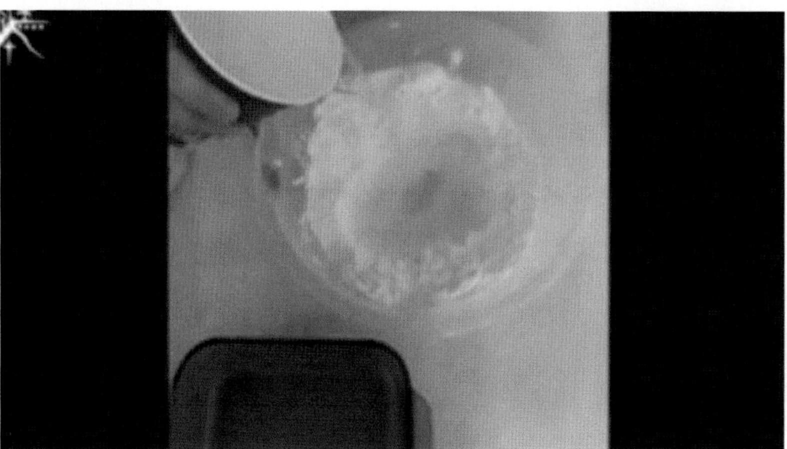

Spoon the flour mixture into the water from the edges of your well to mix it.

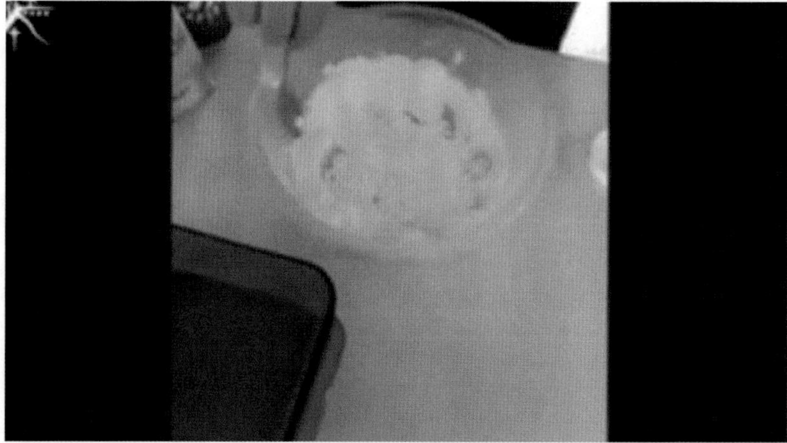

There's going to be dry flour on the outside, but in the middle, you're going to have a wet mixture of the water and the flour coming together. Mix it until it gets bubbly and the flour is not drying. Don't add all the water at all at once. Take your time with it. Look for the bubbles in your mixture.

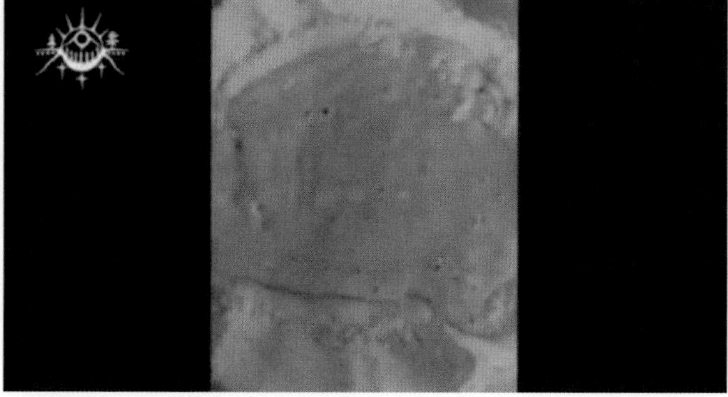

Keep spooning the flour mixture into the water and add a bit more water to it. Make sure the flour's slowly coming into the middle, not putting it all in at once. Some people refer to bannock as hockey pucks, which is what happens when you mix it too quickly.

"If you have clean hands at the end of making your bannock, then it's not properly done."

Don't be afraid to get your hands dirty. Keep mixing until the mixture looks like this:

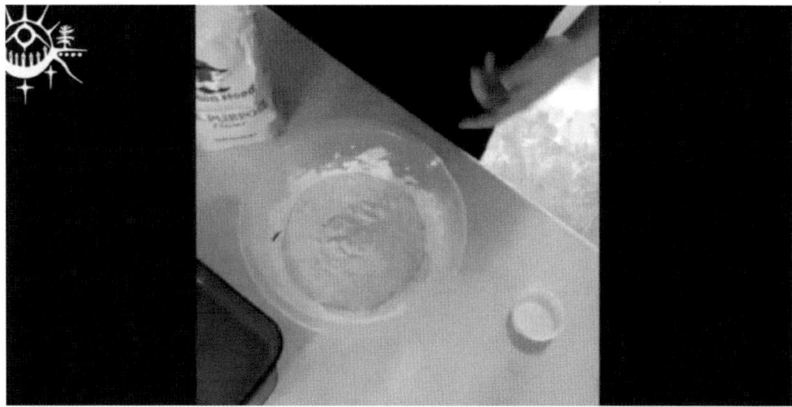

Add extra flour around the edges. Until it looks like this:

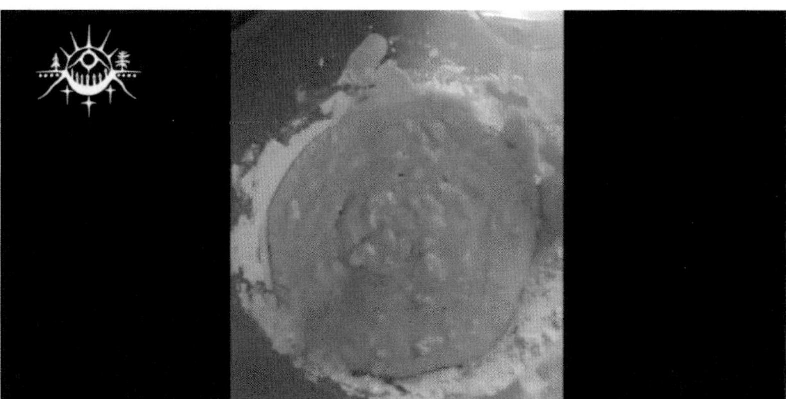

Using your hands, fold the flour over:

Go slow. You don't have to go fast. Keep folding it over in circular motions. The mixing process is slow but it will produce fluffier, tastier bannock.

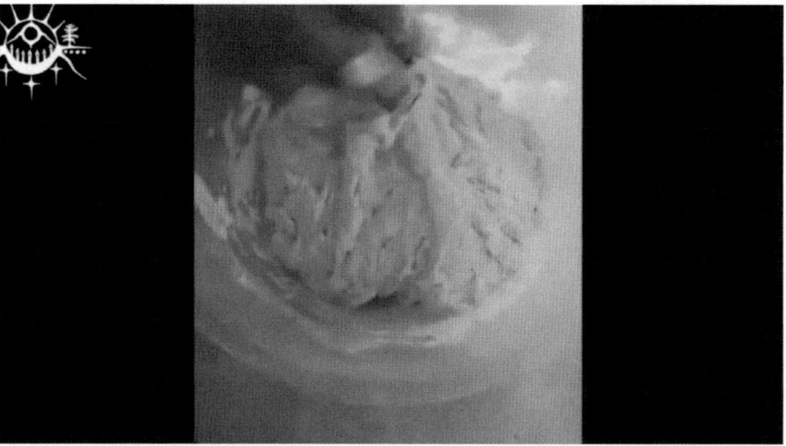

All the flour underneath you're going to want to bring to the top. Add more flour to around the edges.

Keep folding the flour in until it starts to get dry on top. If it's still wet on top when you're folding it over, you need to add more flour. While we suggested 3 cups of flour initially, that amount will change and you need to keep adding to it.

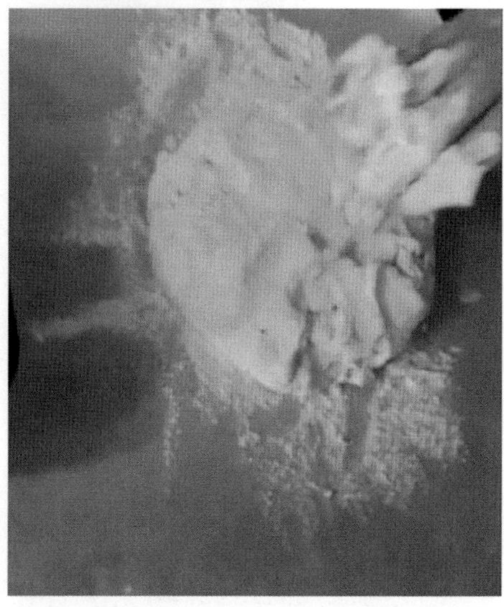

Form it into a large ball of dough and then put it on a surface that has flour on it. That flour will help your bannock not stick to the counter.

This is what your bannock should look like:

It should feel soft and moist but dry on top. Your hands are probably pretty messy at this point.

For fry bread, cut off chunks to fry. Because this project is going to be bannock for the oven, put the dough in a pan.

It will rise a bit in the oven, but it's ready to bake:

This is a family recipe that has been passed down for generations.

After baking, the bannock is ready to eat. You can top it with butter if you like.

Enjoy! How will you eat your bannock?

SO YOU WANNA BE AN ACTOR

Anna Lambe

View the videos in this series online! Scan the QR code, or visit http://www.tigurl.org/beactor

Anna Lambe is an Inuk actress known for portraying Spring in The Grizzlies and Sarah in the CBC mini-series Trickster. She has graciously offered to share her some tips and some things that she wishes she knew before she got involved in the film industry.

"There's so much talent and there's so much creativity within our communities that we need to share with the world. We want to share with the world. We want to share with each other as Indigenous peoples."

Anna Lambe is an Inuk actress known for portraying Spring in The Grizzlies and Sarah in the CBC mini-series Trickster. She has graciously offered to share her some tips and some things that she wishes she knew before she got involved in the film industry.

LESSON ONE: WHERE TO START GETTING INVOLVED IN THE FILM INDUSTRY

There are many entry points to get involved in the acting industry, whether you start as an extra, background or whether you audition for those big roles right away.

"I started as Spring in the Grizzlies, which was not a lead role, but a supporting role, which I later got nominated for best supporting actress. So I think that goes to show you can start all the way at the bottom and work your way up, or sometimes these things happen where you get involved right into the thick of it right away."

HERE ARE ANNA'S TIPS FOR GETTING INVOLVED IN THE ACTING INDUSTRY:

"I know for myself, I wish I had more experience on a set."

Keep an eye out for calls for extras within your community, and calls for extras within the region. Being an extra is a great entry point, it gives you experience, lets you build your resume and gives you experience on set.

"I know for myself, when I saw the opportunity for trickster, it was actually posted by the director, Michelle Latimer on Facebook. I told myself I wasn't going to do it. I wasn't going to do it. Grizzlies was a fluke. And then the day before casting closed, I asked for the sides. I did the audition, I think that morning and sent it in that afternoon."

Be conscious of the opportunities that are coming up and don't be afraid to take them. Try it out, you have nothing to lose! People seeing your face in the application process helps get you out there and helps people get to know you.

"I look back and I'm like, if I had never taken that one opportunity that I saw on Facebook of all places, I wouldn't be in this position that I'm in now."

Find a community that supports you, that uplifts you, that empowers you and that helps get your name out for opportunities or shows you opportunities that you might be suitable for. Rejection can be hard and having people to encourage you can offset that. With a circle of friends, you can create your own projects and get exposed to opportunities you might not have known about otherwise.

Having a community is really important and it really makes all the difference in the world when it comes to feeling supported. And when it comes to feeling like even when the roles are slow and business is slow, when you feel like you're struggling the most, these are the people that are gonna support you and they're gonna uplift you and remind you of why you wanted to do acting, why you wanted to be an actor.

Take advantage of workshops, training and keep improving your skills. You will feel more confident in auditions if you do.

"It doesn't make you any less of an actor or any less serious because the big name actors, they still do drama classes."

Leverage the power of social media. Use it to share your work and get your art out there.

"These social media communities can really get your name out there further can connect you with more people and can show you opportunities that you've never seen before. I feel like the film and television industry is so interconnected through social media and a lot of the interactions that are happening now are through social media."

Be realistic and manage your expectations. Don't expect huge roles immediately. The industry is highly competitive.

"Sometimes I feel like we get too hopeful and we let ourselves down, we start at the beginning of the year and our new year's resolution is 'I want to book a lead role this year' and sometimes it doesn't happen and that's okay."

Don't expect your journey to be linear and that you are going to move from background to supporting to lead.

"Sometimes you go from supporting to a lead to supporting again, and it can kind of get you down on your confidence a little bit, but you're not going to be the lead in everything. Even the most skilled person in the world is not the lead in everything."

Don't give up. Your next role might be right around the corner. Keep trying, keep trying out and keep looking out for those opportunities. Keep being you and keep confidence in yourself.

"Grizzlies came to me when I least expected it, Trickster came to me when I least expected it. I never thought that I was going to get involved in this industry, but here I am. There's a lot of opportunities, especially for us as Indigenous actors right now, where we want to tell our stories, people want to hear our stories and there's that extra support for the Indigenous film and television industry."

Such powerful advice from such a powerful actress! Do you feel inspired about your film career?

LESSON 2: AUDITIONS

In this lesson, Anna Lambe shares her best audition tips about how to set up for a good audition. This lesson couldn't come at a better time especially with the eyes on Indigenous film and television and how many casting calls are happening for different projects all across North America. Currently, the pandemic has meant that all auditions happen through self-tape rather than in audition rooms.

HERE ARE ANNA'S TIPS:

Setup for your audition tape is really, really important. In Anna's video lesson she notes that the lighting is a bit harsh on her features and the colour behind her isn't ideal by some people's standards (they would prefer white, blue or something creamy.

Follow Instructions

Look at the requirements in your documentation. Typically they will say if they want waist up, shoulder up or hips up to be captured in your video.

Set Yourself Up To Be Seen

Have a clear camera so the casting director can see your eyes and your emotions. Use a stand for your camera so your video is steady and not shaky.

Sound

Sound is really important. They need to be able to:

- hear you clearly
- understand what you're saying
- Listen to the emotions you're putting into your words
- Take note of you emphasize and don't emphasize

Sound check! Make sure:

- your mic is clear
- it works well

- you can hear everything clearly
- you have no off-putting background noise

Lack of background noise is important because it keeps the casting director from getting distracted so they can focus on your performance.

Lighting
You also want to make sure you place yourself in the best light, literally. You can diffuse overly harsh light with an umbrella like Anna does so it doesn't cast so many shadows. A ring light can be pretty helpful for creating great lighting.

Research
Outside of the lighting and sound, you want to make sure you do your homework for the action audition.

Take a deep dive into

- whatever the audition scene that you're doing is
- what could come before in the scene
- what comes after
- what are your intentions when you're doing the scene?
- what is the backstory of the character that you're trying to portray
- how you want to embody this character
- how you think they would react and respond
- what you think the story is
- all the different aspects of this character that you want to portray
- whatever takes that you have on this character

To get ready, make sure you read the character's description and do an in-depth analysis of your character and of the scene. Doing that makes all the difference in your performance and will show through in the emotions that you portray, in the way that you respond to people and in the character as a whole. Put a lot of thought into what your performance is going to be.

"You want to engage with the person that you are performing with and you want to be immersed in the scene and not constantly having to look down to find out what your next line is. "

Be As Off Book As Possible
Try to have the emotions and the vibe of the scene, along with all the words, before you even get in front of the camera.

BEING OFF BOOK:

you know all the words, the emotions you're trying to portray and what the scene is about

"You want to make sure that the clothes that you're wearing are flattering, that they fit the character, that they look good on camera and that they make you look and feel good in your performance. Same goes with hair."

Be Presentable

Consult your audition documentation for any specific instructions about hair, makeup or wardrobe.

Think about:

- How are you going to dress?
- How are you going to do your makeup?
- How are you going to do your hair?

Putting It All Together

"Once you step in front of that camera, just have fun, show all that analysis and all that hard work that you put on behind the scenes, show that in front of the camera...do your audition with passion and with confidence and you'll feel proud of the work that you do... All those extra steps that you take, all those extra notes that you take, they are noticeable and people see it."

The extra effort is worth it, so do your homework and feel good about what you're bringing to the table.

Give Yourself Some Grace

"I know sometimes when we're doing auditions, sometimes we can get really intense and we mess up one thing when an audition is going really well and then we get super hard on ourselves. That doesn't help anyone."

Don't be too hard on yourself. If you're freaking out, you're probably also upsetting your reader. You can record as many times as you need to for a self-tape. Be gentle with yourself and try to enjoy the process.

Anna's Pep Talk:

"I believe in you. And I think that if you take all these extra steps you will have a great audition and you will be remembered by the casting director or anybody who saw your audition video."

Do you feel ready for the audition now?

LESSON 3: SELF CARE IN THE FILM AND TELEVISION INDUSTRY

"There's just this expectation that... acting can't be that hard of a job, but acting can be really mentally, emotionally, and physically taxing. Sometimes we drain ourselves so much while we give all of ourselves to others."

Self-care is so important in the film and television industry, particularly in Indigenous film.

"We're covering so many really hurtful topics, really sensitive topics that a lot of us experienced personally, such as suicide or domestic violence or different depictions or manifestations of intergenerational trauma. This seems to be a common factor in a lot of Indigenous film and television."

The themes addressed in Indigenous film can feel particularly heavy and that's why taking care of yourself is so crucial.

Decide What You Want To Do

"We see a lot of people within our communities creating these stories, or a lot of the time we see people from outside our communities, writing these stories about Indigenous people that oftentimes have these stereotypical roles or really sensitive and really emotional and really like mentally draining roles."

What choices do you have as an actor to take care of yourself in these situations?

"I want to address first: don't feel obligated to take these roles, to audition for these roles, just because you need to work. If it's something that you think is too sensitive for you, if you think it's something that's going to really hurt you to portray, and there's, you know, aspects of these roles that you don't really like, or you feel like they're not representative of you and not just of you, but of your beliefs and your feelings towards Indigenous representation, then don't feel obligated to take these roles, know that you can say no, at the end of the day, we have to face ourselves in the mirror."

Having boundaries around what you will and won't do is part of taking care of yourself.

"There are going to be times where we have to take tough roles or you have to take roles that maybe they weren't our favorite, but they didn't compromise our moral compass."

Routine

The other piece that's important for self care is establishing a routine. Being able to disconnect from the roles you play at the end of the day is so important. Plan what you want to do at the end of the day so that you're doing something just for you, whether that's cooking, exercise or something else you enjoy.

Mental Health

"Another really important part of self care in the film and television industry is frequently and consistently checking in with yourself, checking in with your mental health, checking in with your confidence, checking in with your self esteem, because in this industry, it can be really tough."

Rejection, disappointment and feeling relentless scrutiny of physical appearance can be tough. Having a platform can come with a lot of pressure.

Ask yourself:

- Where are you at mentally?
- Are you really, really struggling?
- Are you in a pretty good place?
- Do you think you could be doing better so that you can address that immediately?

Make sure to address things that are impacting your self-confidence.

Body Image

Do you feel like you're putting a lot of pressure on yourself to look a certain way?

"Your body takes care of you. If you're not happy with where your body's at right now, because you don't feel good, then, you know, do what makes you feel good. But if you are having really low confidence or self esteem, just because you feel like you're not skinny enough, you're not good looking enough. That's not a good place to be in."

There's making choices that support your wellness and there's making choices for unhealthy reasons due to pressure and other people's goals for your body.

"It's perfectly okay to want to change how you look or how you feel, because it's not where you feel your best, but once you start wanting to change how you look, because you're like, 'Oh, I don't like the way I look on camera' or 'I feel like I'm not skinny enough to be getting these roles.' Then you need to address that. That's a really unhealthy view of yourself and that can lead to further damage down the road."

Perspective

"The other really important form of self care is being able to differentiate between constructive criticism and just hate."

People will give a lot of advice about acting, how to get further involved, or how to level up. Criticism isn't all bad.

"Constructive criticism can really help your career and can really help you as an actor. But sometimes people will just say mean things just because they want to say mean things or because they don't know how to properly get their point across and it just comes across as hateful."

Being able to tell the difference between constructive criticism helps you apply valid critique and also shapes how you feel about yourself after you receive it. Constructive criticism helps you improve. Hate just makes you feel bad (and you can just throw it away!)

Boundaries

"Respecting your boundaries is just as important as setting them."

Anna did not at first honour her own boundaries around social media when she got started and she faced harassment over her choice not to engage with every person who interacted with her on social media.

Managing Expectations

"Manage your expectations of how quickly you're going to grow in this industry and the different opportunities that are going to come your way."

Anna has a vision board of what she wants for the future but she manages her expectations because disappointment hits her hard.

"It's really important that we have dreams and we have goals and we have visions, but also be really careful that you don't get your hopes up super, super high."

Handling Rejection

Learning how to handle rejection is so key. It's an important piece of self-care.

"There's going to be a lot of nos in this industry. You get a lot of no's and sometimes you don't even get no's. You just never hear from a casting director, again, be prepared for that. Be prepared that you're not going to

get every audition, even the audition that you put so much time and energy into, and that you put your everything into it. It doesn't always work out."

Working hard is no guarantee you will get a role and that has to be okay.

"Some opportunities just aren't meant to be and that's okay at the end of the day you can't really change that. You can't change the fact that you're not the right person for a role."

Ultimately, getting a no isn't an indictment of your talent and it's crucial not to take it personally.

"These things are inevitable, but it doesn't mean that you're a bad actor. It doesn't mean that you have no place in this industry. It just means that you're not the right person for that role. Or maybe it's just not your take on the character that they wanted. And that's perfectly fine."

It's not necessarily about you, it's just something that comes with the job.

"It's not a measure of your self-worth, it's not a measure of your worth as an actor. It's just an inevitable aspect of the industry that none of us as actors can escape. Don't let it define your worth."

Take care of yourself, you're worth it!

LESSON 4: WHAT ANNA WISHES SHE KNEW

"As a young person I never really expected that I could be an actor that the opportunity would ever come up to be an actor. So I never really had any aspirations to be an actor. I wish as a young person, I knew how many entry points there were into acting, whether you want to do acting seriously or not."

So Many Ways To Get In

The reality is there are many entry points to acting. You could start:

- as an extra
- with a drama class
- with a workshop

There are other ways to get involved with film that aren't acting, like behind the camera work, writing, directing, producing, working as a counter person, grip, or a set decorator.

The Speed of the Industry

"The other thing that was really unexpected was like the speed at which the film and television industry works. Iit's super, super slow. It's weeks before you hear back from somebody. You did an audition the last week of November and you hear back the first week of January, and they're like, 'All right, we want a call back, be ready for three days from now."

Anna knows all about the patience and flexibility required in working in an industry that runs on its own time.

"Things can happen super, super fast when sometimes things take a really long time. Manage your expectations on when you're going to hear something; don't give up hope on certain projects."

Anna suggests not losing hope on a role unless you hear they have started filming.

"The film and television industry is really competitive, but your experience and the people that you surround yourself with, that's really up to you. You can't avoid toxic people in the workplace all the time, but you can choose who you support, who supports you."

The film industry can be cutthroat, but there are things you can do to shape your experience.

"You choose your attitude and your outlook on certain projects that, even the most draining ones, there's always a little bit of light in there."

The perspective you bring to each experience can be a game-changer.

"Before entering this industry, I wish I knew that my experience was what I made. My support groups are what I made them. My peers are who I chose them to be. Yeah, it's competitive. It's fast paced. Sometimes it's really, really tough, but your experience as an actor is what you make it."

You can look back on even tough projects and find moments of fun or moments that were rewarding. You do need to go into things with your eyes open, even if you can reframe when it's all over.

"I wish I knew how to read contracts and I wish I knew my entitlements as an actor. I wish I knew what it meant to be ACTRA and what it meant to be Non-ACTRA. These are things that I still don't completely understand, but I have an agent now that helps me understand these different things."

Just like preparing for your audition, preparing to fulfil your contract takes some homework.

"I wish I had taken the extra steps to know what everything means in a contract, what my obligations are."

Anna shared how she was so well-taken care of on Trickster, but would have felt better if she was more familiar with contract language. The good news is, you don't have to navigate that process alone.

"I highly suggest once you get involved in the film television, television industry, once you get your contracts that you reach out to another actor or somebody that you're close with and ask them questions. If you have any questions about your contract... you're allowed to ask questions, know that you can ask, you can figure things out."

Anna says it's so important to learn:

- how to read a contract
- how to ask questions
- who you can ask questions to

Agents can be so helpful and their role is really important.

"These people, they are your advocates in the film and television industry, they are your advocates. When you're entering productions, they are the people who are fighting to protect your rights as an actor, who understand what's in a contract, what's in the film and television industry, what you're obligated to."

Anna wishes she had got herself an agent after finishing The Grizzlies because their work is so crucial. Having someone who speaks your language is so valuable.

"It's made me more comfortable that my agent is able to handle all the legal stuff and they're able to explain things to me in plain English and not legal documents."

Understanding your role in relation to what's happening around you is also important. Context is key.

"As an actor, people on sets and those sorts of things, they're going to treat you like the center of the universe, but at the end of the day, you are not the center of the universe. Even in a lead role, you're not the center of a universe. You're not even really the center of production. There's so many aspects that come into filming a TV show or a movie and there's so many interconnected things that to say that the actor is like the heart of a production, it's wrong."

Your attitude about where you fit in is also something to consider.

"It's not fair to kind of have this sort of entitlement or attitude when you're on set. You're not the center of the universe. People might treat you like it, but be humble, have humility, just be a kind person."

Things Don't Just End At The Wrap Of Production

Be aware that there are things that will generally come after production and post-production. You still have ADR, which is where you go and rerecord lines that may have been compromised by background noise on set.

Be prepared

Planning for your financial future and present is something that needs to happen for you to thrive.

"The acting industry isn't always super fruitful. Make sure that you have a backup plan or a side hustle that you make money with or something that sustains your life because that's really important. You're not going to get every audition. You're not going to get every role. Sometimes things are quiet for a long, long time. Know what you can do and what you want to do outside of the industry and know that you need something to support yourself in the time being."

Keep An Open Mind

Where you start in the film industry isn't necessarily where you will end up.

"When I got into the film and television industry, I thought I was only going to be an actor. I only wanted to act. I didn't think there was any path outside of that, like what skills from acting can you apply to other jobs? But this experience in film and television you can extend outside of your roles. If you want to do writing, if you want to do directing, if you want to do producing, there's all these different things."

If you decide to do something different, you wouldn't be the first actor to decide that and you won't be the last!

"You can move within the industry and you can kind of pursue different career paths if acting doesn't feel right for you, or if you need a different creative outlet. There's a lot of very versatile and multi talented actors out there who are also directors, who are also producers, who maybe started off as actors and went into directing or who wanted to direct and then went into acting. There's a lot of room for movement within this industry."

You have a unique perspective to be able to see what opportunities are available to you and expand your horizons.

"As an actor, we get to see a lot of what's happening behind the scenes. If there's something that interests you, pursue it, especially if you have an agent that works with an agency that also does writing or represents directors. Talk with your agent about wanting to expand or explore."

Ultimately, the film industry is an amazing opportunity and one Anna treasures.

"It's a lot of fun. I love acting. I feel like there's so much potential for people to share their stories. We have so many amazing up and coming creatives, so many established creatives. This industry is ours. It's what we make it at this point. I'm really excited to see what comes out of Indigenous talent."

Anna's journey has been incredible and yours could be too. Whatever happens, it's your path!

"There's so many different stories and I'm sure your story is going to be different as well, but I wish you the best in getting involved in acting."

Now get out there and pursue your acting dreams!

ACTING WITH DANA KHAN (JEFFREY)

Dana Khan (Jeffrey) is an accomplished artist who hasn't stopped working hard on her career, appearing in multiple television shows, commercials, and dance appearances.

She is Guyanese and Ojibwe from Selkirk, Manitoba, but now lives in Mississauga, Ontario, and has been doing work as a performing artist in both acting and dancing. She is also the youth coordinator of an organization called Toronto Council Fire Native Cultural Centre, and coordinator of the First Fire Dance Program.

Dana says a big part of her life was starting the First Fire Dance Program at Council Fire, which is a program for ages seven all the way up into early adulthood with different styles of dance taught.

"We're telling stories through our movement is what I'm trying to say. We talked about missing and murdered Indigenous women. We've talked about the residential school system, what it means to reclaim our culture through our dances," said Dana.

Amongst teaching dance, she's appeared in TV shows like Anne with an E and performed in a music video for a band called Crown Lands.

"Being a performing artist has opened up a lot of doors, with acting and dance and teaching, it's really led me in different directions."

Dana's journey to the performing arts was something she says, "chose her" and was always dancing, always wanted to perform, and had a love for storytelling.

"I feel like that was just in my blood and it is part of who we are as Indigenous people, we're storytellers. So it was just a natural evolution," said Dana.

She also says dance and performing arts helped her through a "really, really dark time" in her life and says it was a way to heal and express herself without having to do so verbally.

Although dance and performing was a natural instinct for her, Dana still went to school and calls her journey both informal and formal.

She started dancing with going to the Royal Winnipeg Ballet School and went on to York University where she did her fine arts degree focused in dance and was training in ballet, contemporary, modern jazz, and more.

As for the acting, she says it was "pretty informal."

"At first, it was just watching videos, getting inspired, watching TV. Honestly, when I was younger, I would look at scripts and I would practice them in the mirror," said Dana.

But in order to do what she wanted to do as a performer, she had to leave her home in Manitoba and move to a big city in another province. She says it was "really, really hard" but what helped her with the transition was staying connected to friends back home and joining groups and connecting with people who had similar interests.

Dana has faced other obstacles within her career of course. Being a performing artist, she says she faces rejection constantly and has moments of self-doubt if performing is the career for her.

"What really helped me was knowing that, to be an artist, it's not just because someone says yes or someone tells you you're good. It's about the process; it's about the love for it. If you love your art, then you're on the right path."

In fact, her process to get on the show "Anne with an E" took time. Dana had auditioned many times for the show and was told no, then got a call to audition and didn't think much of it because she heard no "so many times."

She got a callback, and had to do many other auditions which she called "an audition marathon" and wasn't sure if she was going to get through.

"When I got the job, I got the call, I was over the moon. I was like, "What? This is amazing." Anne with an E was in a really incredible storyline that touched on the residential school system, and it was really portrayed in an honest way, and it was a really amazing experience," said Dana.

When performing, community inspires her and "seeing our people" reclaim language and culture, but also inspired by those that came before her and paved the way to where she is today.

"I feel like when I see actors on TV, like Michael Greyeyes, I say, 'Whoa,' I get so excited, I'm like that's so inspiring and if he could do it, maybe I can do it," said Dana.

"It's like seeing people paving the way and then also knowing that maybe my journey is paving the way for others."

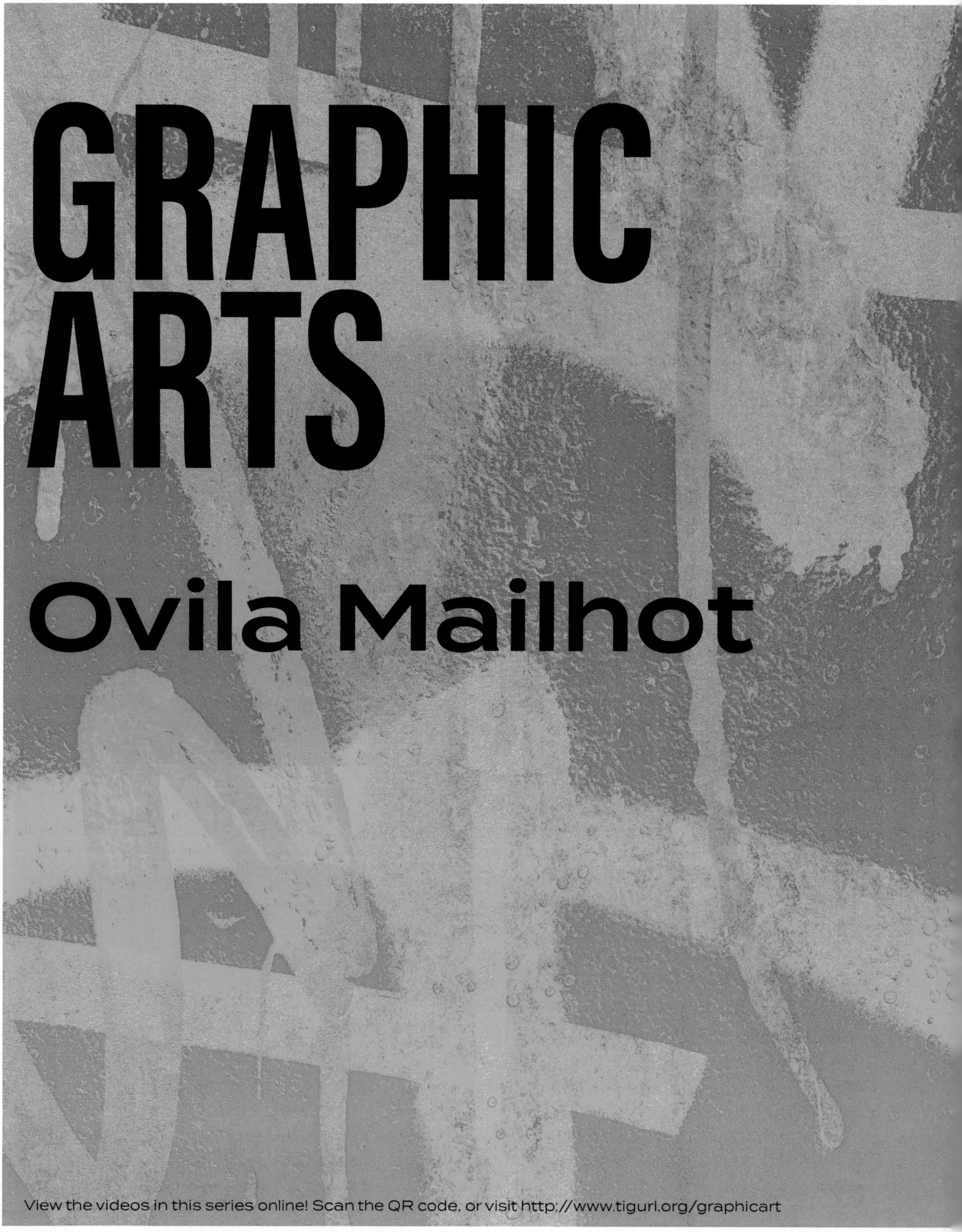

GRAPHIC ARTS

Ovila Mailhot

View the videos in this series online! Scan the QR code, or visit http://www.tigurl.org/graphicart

Ovila Mailhot, a Coast Salish graphic artist originally from Seabird Island, British Columbia, has put together a graphic art tutorial to share his gifts. Follow along to learn how to make great digital art.

LESSON 1: PHOTOSHOP BASICS

Ovila has been doing graphic art for six years and learned his craft through YouTube tutorials that covered Photoshop and illustrator. Inspired by those he learned from and the vision of Indigenous creators sharing their tips and tricks, Ovila created this resource to help other aspiring artists.

MIRRORING AN IMAGE: CREATING A SYMMETRICAL DESIGN

This is a Cosalish hummingbird design that Ovila did recently. He already drew it out, added some editing to it, a little bit of shadowing and a drop shadow effect. He decided he wanted to add onto this.

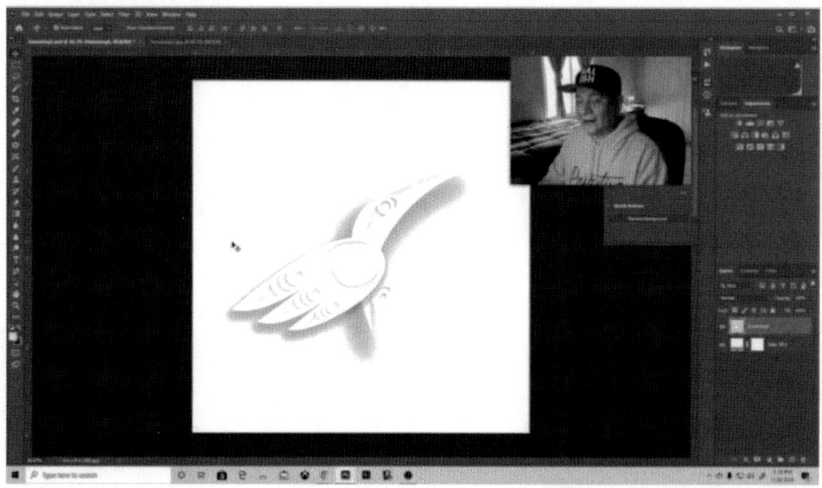

Step 1. Create guidelines. Go to view and make sure the following items are checked:

- Rulers
- Snap
- Snap to guides

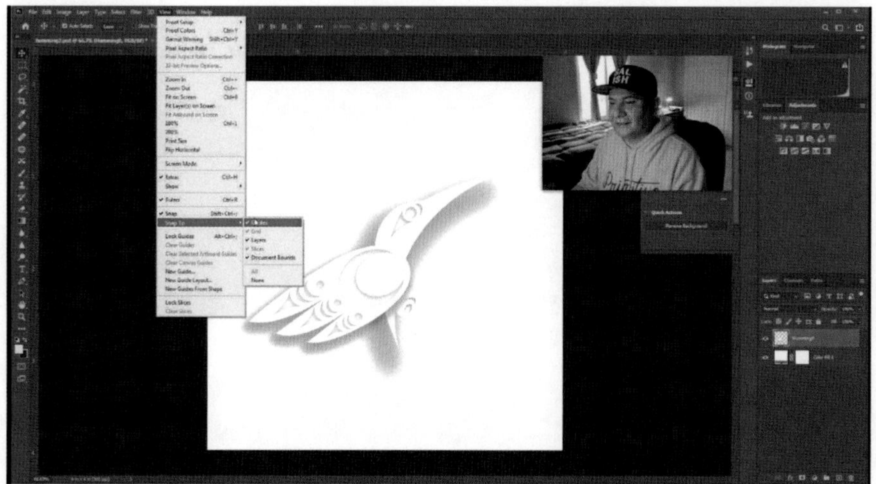

What that means is when you pull that ruler over from the left, it's going to snap in place in the center of the page. The result is the blue line you see in the middle.

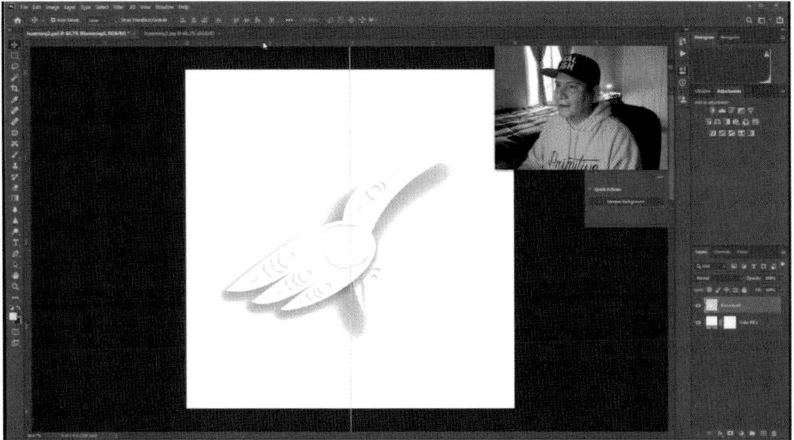

Pull another one down from the top to find the centre of your canvas.

Press Control T on a PC to select the image. Rotate it while holding the shift button to angle it vertically.

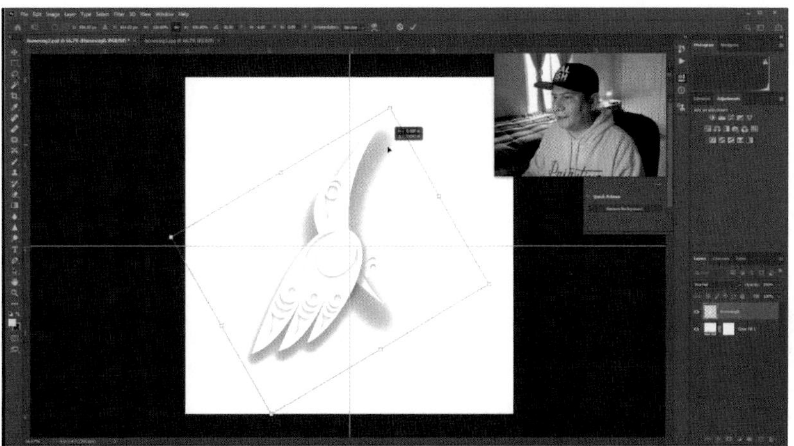

Drag it over beside the center line:

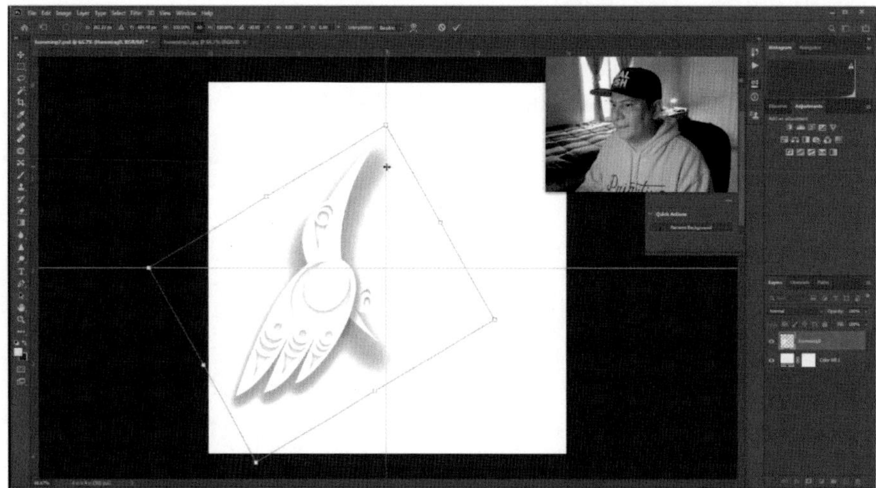

Hit enter, then Control + J to create another hummingbird image on top of it. Press Control + T to select the bird. Right click on the mouse and select 'flip horizontal.'

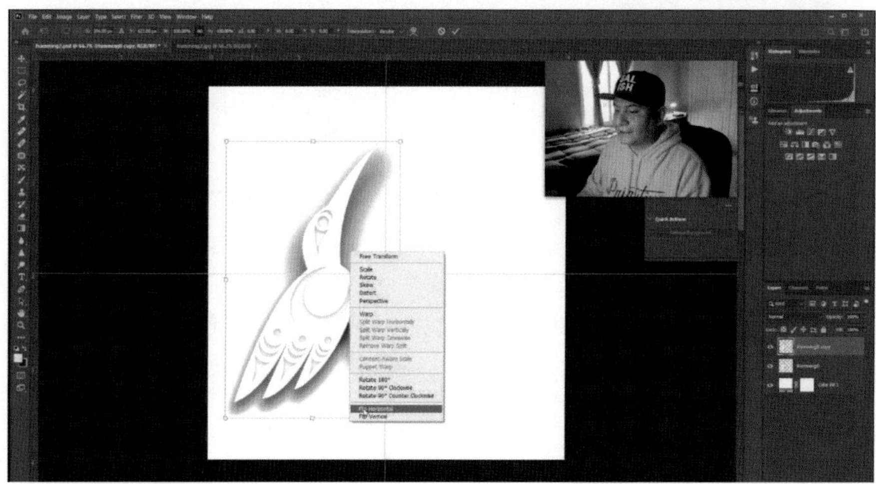

Drag it over to the other side of the canvas.

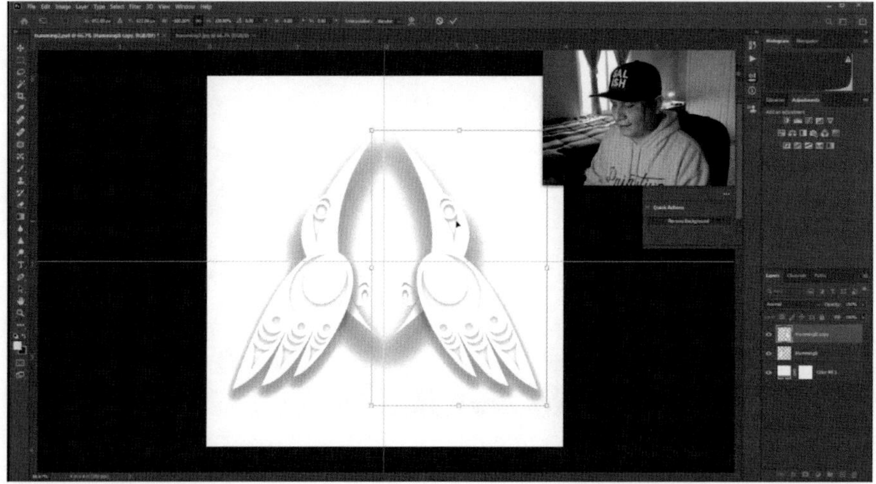

Hit Enter. Add another layer. Using the ellipse tool, add a circle underneath.

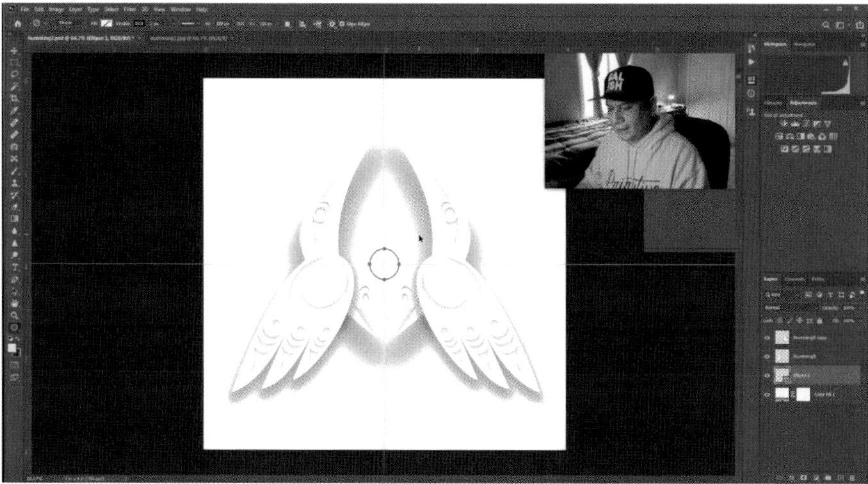

Hit Control + T to select it and expand it while holding the alt key.

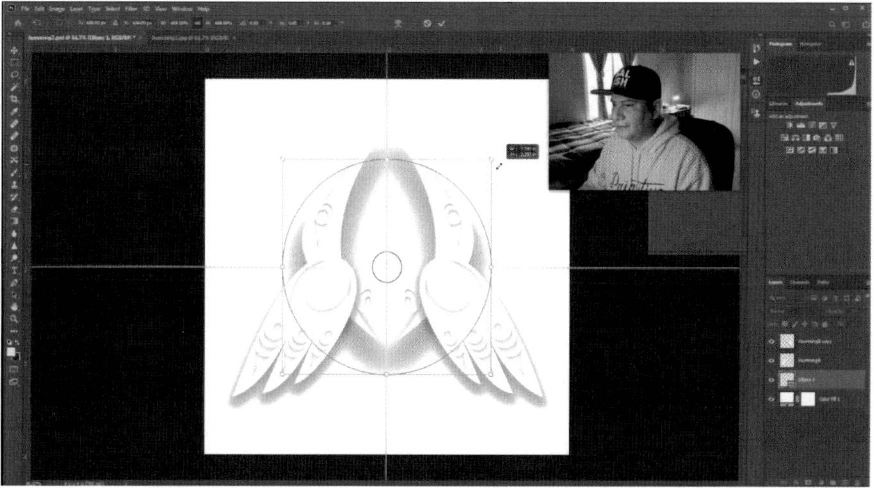

Add some colour:

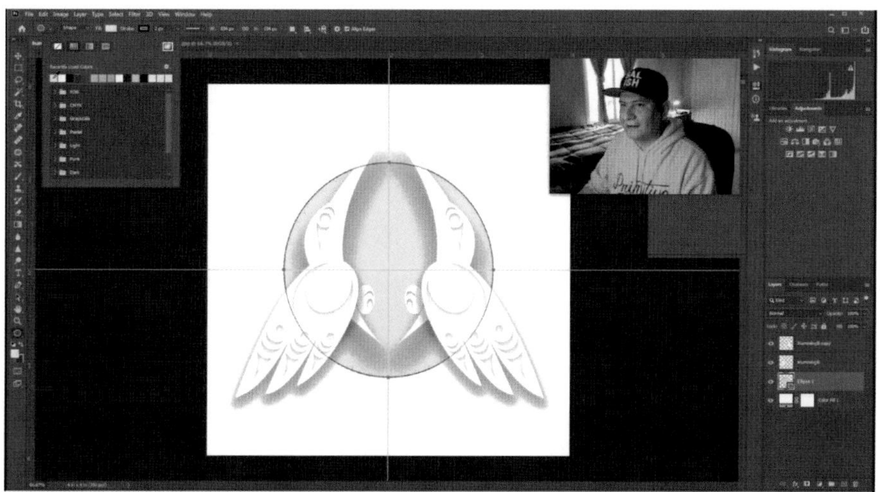

Adjust the placement of the circle behind by dragging it upwards.

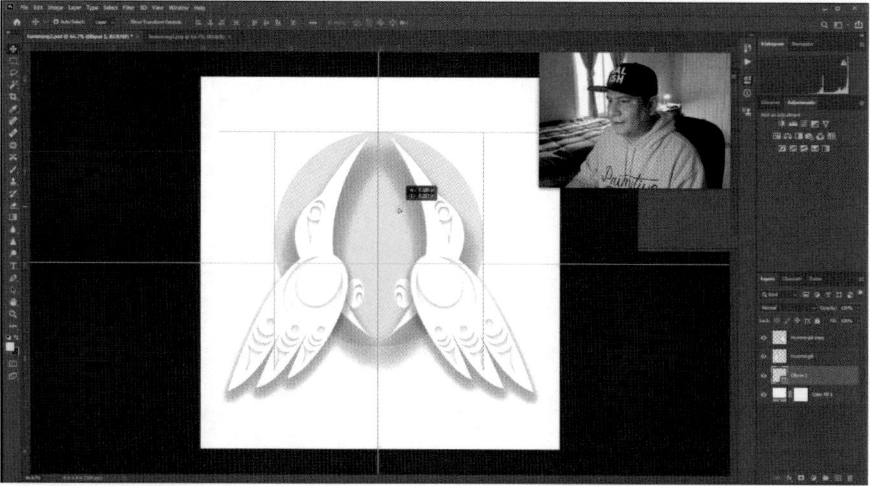

This was the final design Ovila created:

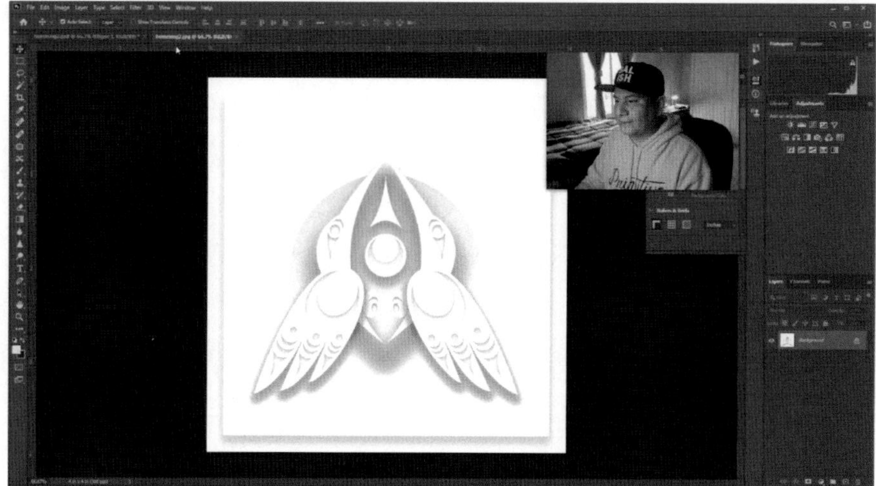

LESSON 2: ROUGH SKETCH

In this lesson Ovila takes us from rough sketch to cleaned up image. In this lesson Ovila will be making a Coast Salish Eagle design. Typically Ovila does his rough sketches in ArtRage and transfers them to Photoshop. He will be using the paint symmetry function which you can access here:

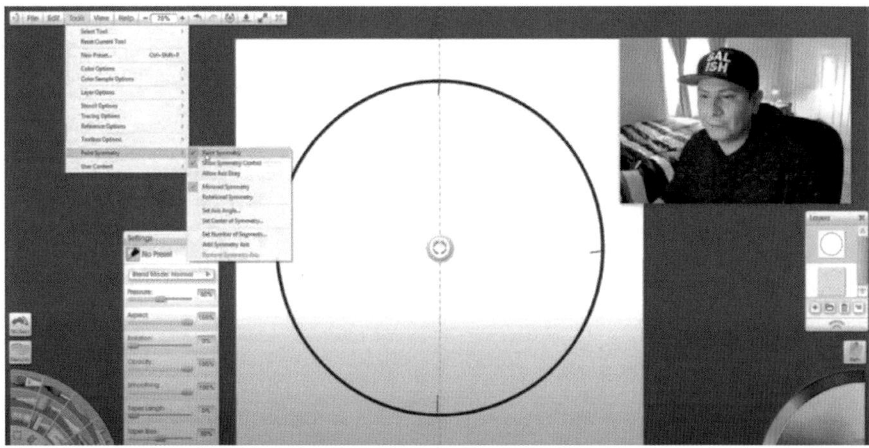

With that turned on, anything he draws on one side will be duplicated in the other. Select the image with control + A, hit Control + C to copy it and Control + V to paste it into a Photoshop canvas.

Next, he lowered the opacity to 20.

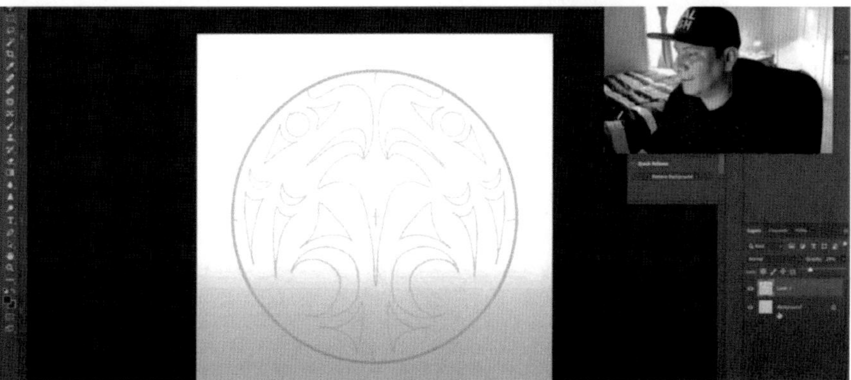

Next, add another layer with and with the ellipse tool, create another outline, expanding the ellipse to the right size:

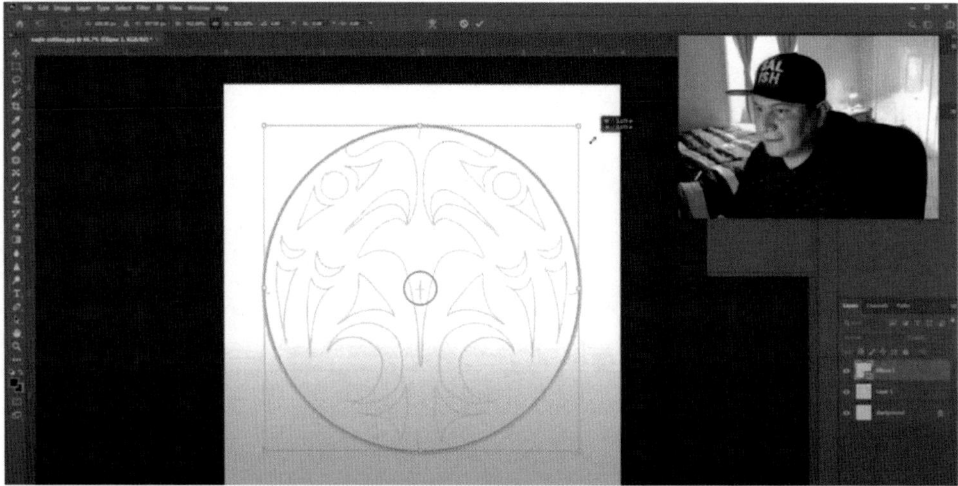

Use the pen tool to create the body outline:

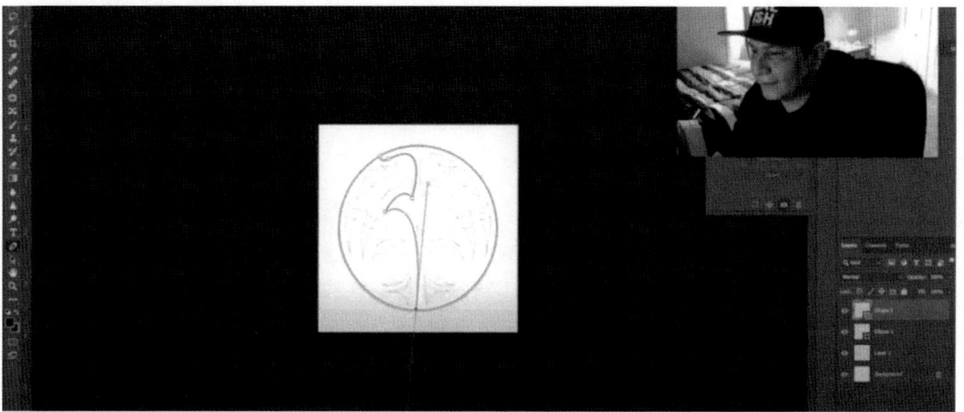

Make a new layer and go over the rest of your lines. You can also duplicate shapes with Control + J:

"Using the pen tool has saved me so much time, as opposed to when I used to draw with stencils and rulers and trying to make everything look nice."

Here's how you can use an ellipse to create an outline over a circle:

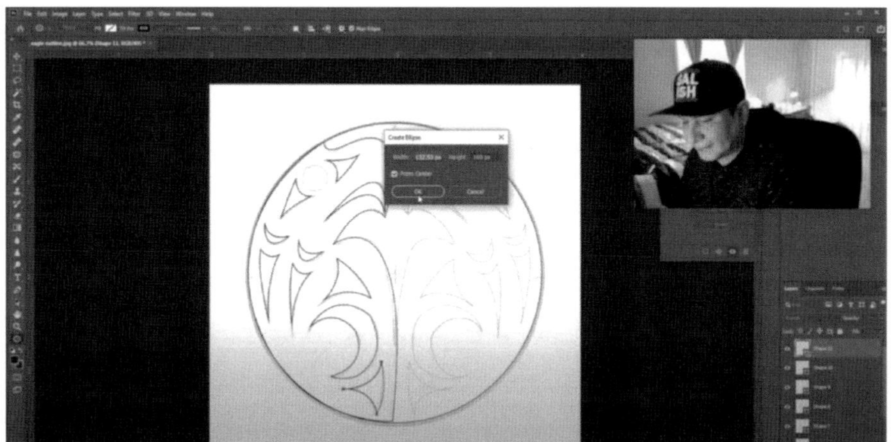

Expand it or shrink it as needed to go over your sketched circle.

Continue outlining your design: When you turn the rough sketch invisible, you get a cleaner design:

Use Colour Fill on the body to make it red:

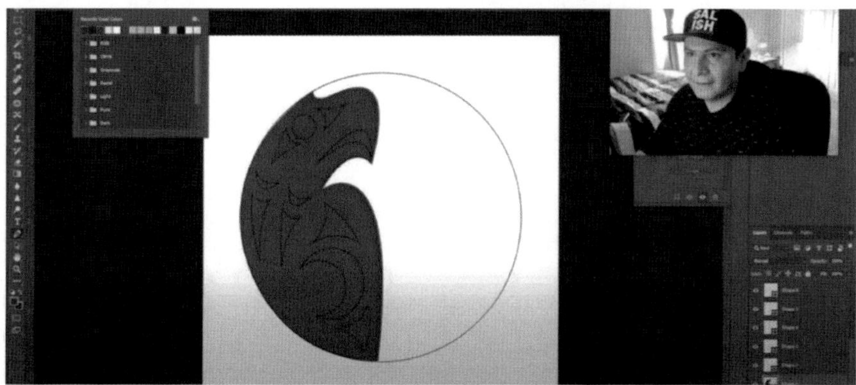

Group the outlined shapes together using Control + E:

Make those black using the Colour Fill:

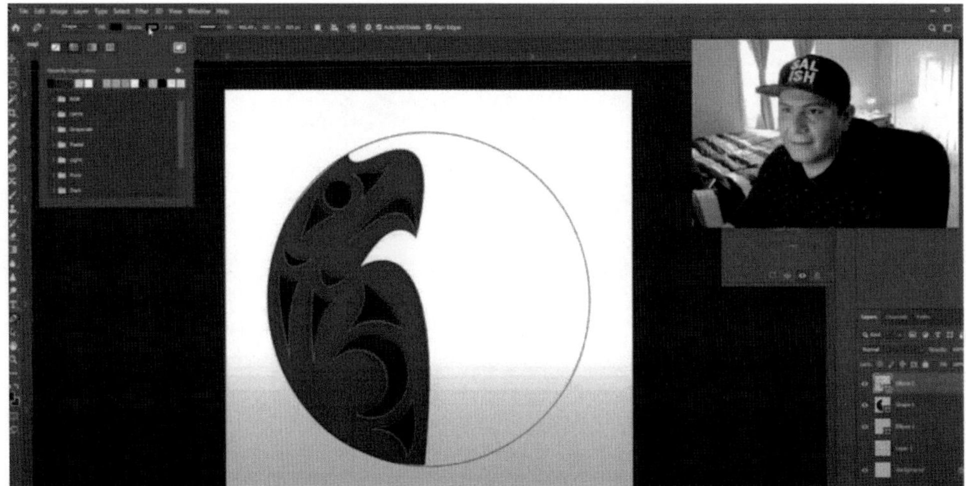

Hit Control + J to make a copy, Control T and Flip Vertical to duplicate the image as a mirror like we did in the last lesson. Here's the result:

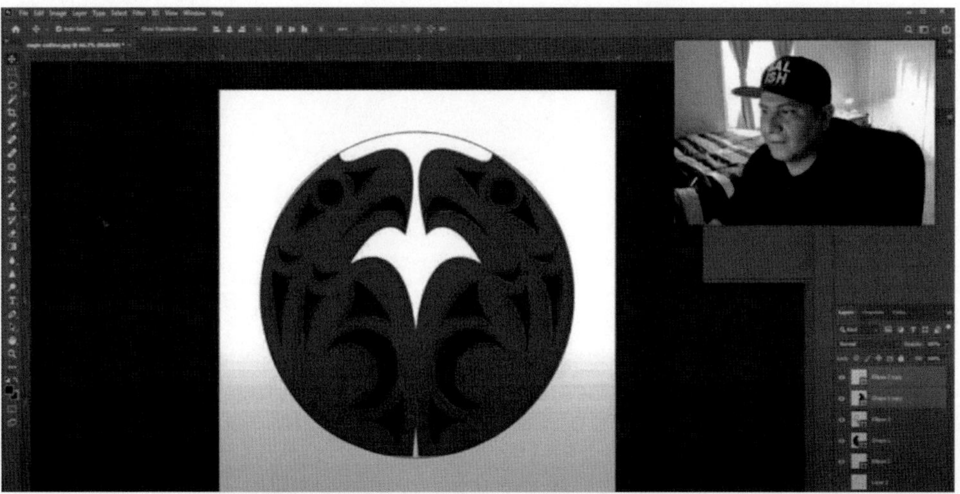

Use the Colour Fill tool to make the background black:

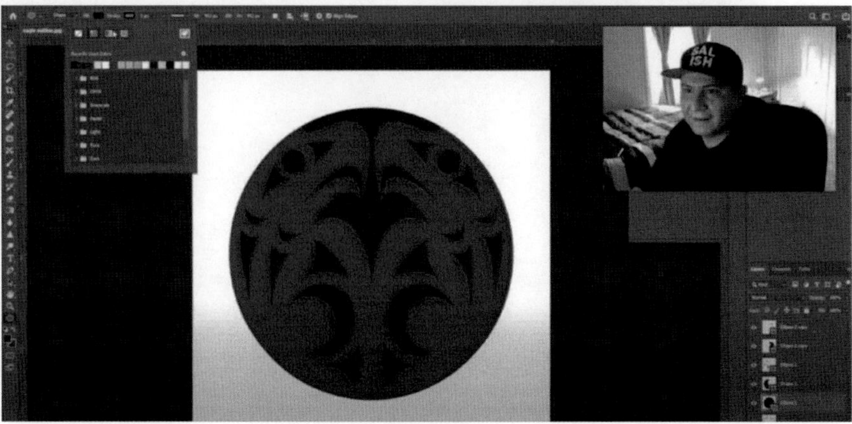

LESSON 3: CLEAR IMAGE

In this lesson we will be cleaning up a rough sketch and turning it into a clear image. Start by reducing the opacity to 20%. Outline the sketch using the pen tool. The pen tool uses anchor points to create the shape:

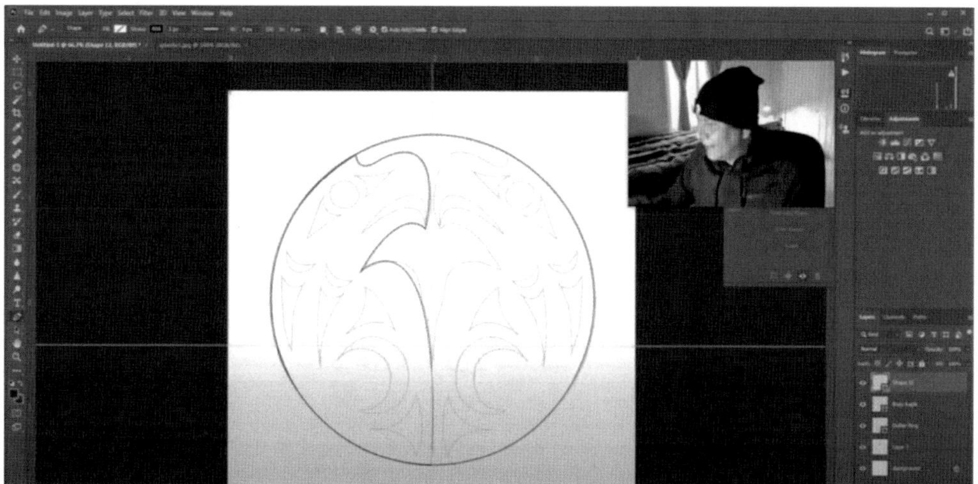

Click and hold down with the mouse and manipulate the curve then click on the other anchor point to trace the shape of the trigon. Use the ellipse tool to create the eye.

Take away the rough sketch:

Group the shapes together using Control + E:

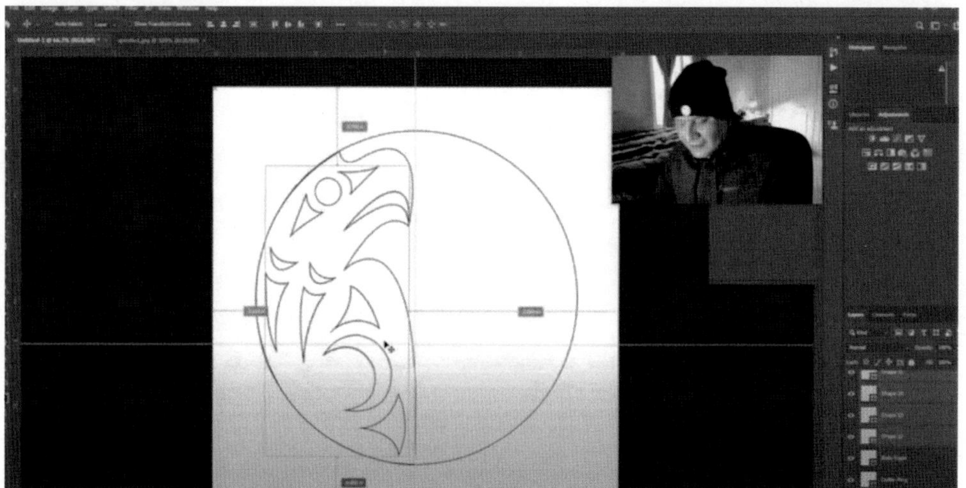

Duplicate and flip the image:

This is what it will look like duplicated:

"When I first started out, I didn't exactly have a teacher. So what I would do is I would look to the history. I would look in books and museum archives, fellow artists would share photos with me, basically looking into the history of our art through our ancestral designs."

This is an example of a Coast Salish spindle whirl:

"When I look at this, it gave me a better understanding of our culture and the history behind it. I'm always doing research. When I look back at these designs, it really helped me develop my own style in the Coast Salish art."

LESSON 4: COLOUR AND GRADIENTS

In this lesson we are going to add colour and gradients to the design we've created. You can start by filling the body outline with black.

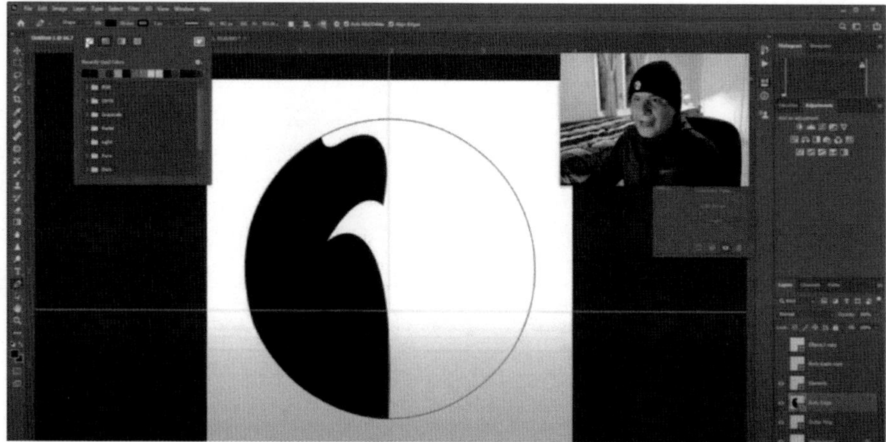

Make the shapes red:

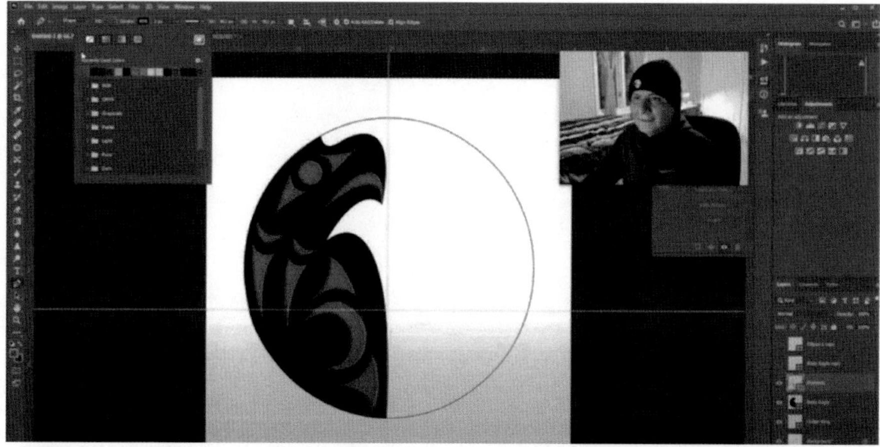

Play around with gradients in the fill by clicking here:

Alternately, click on the layer you want to add gradient to and go to blending options:

Use the gradient tool within blending options to apply a gradient:

Click on the colour point to add a custom colour:

This is the effect it can create:

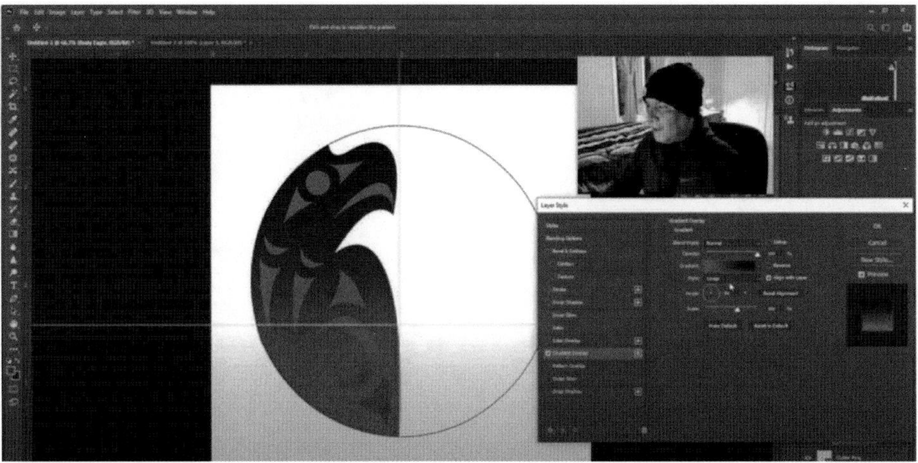

You can add different gradients to each layer:

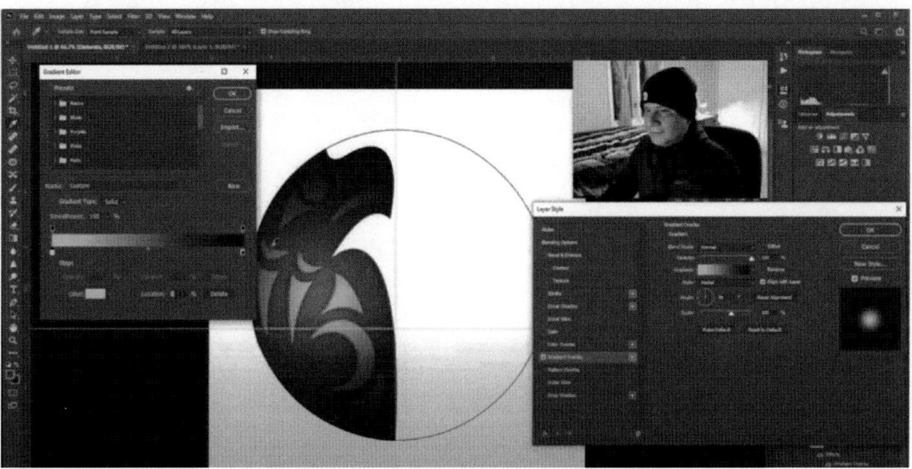

You can add more depth to the image by selecting inner shadow and drop shadow effect to make a cutout effect:

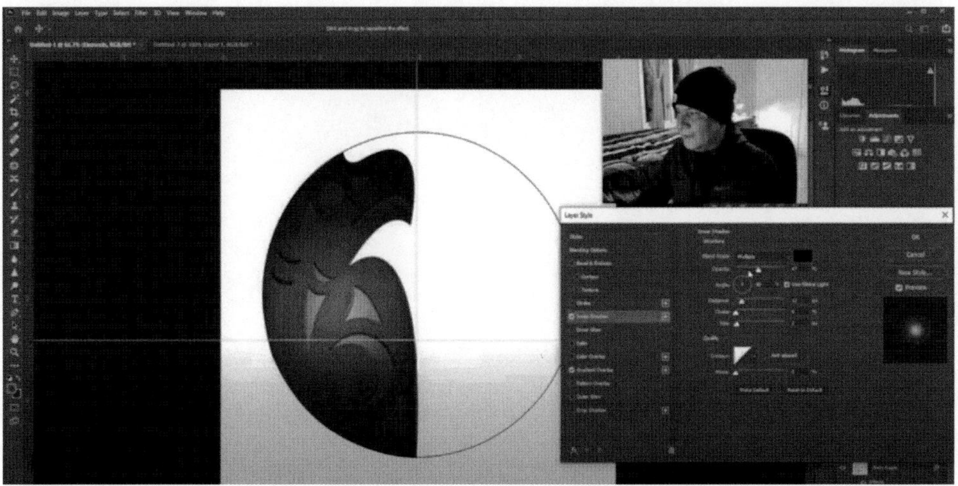

When you're happy with it you can select multiple layers with the shift button, duplicate it with Control + J and Control + T to duplicate the image. You can also change the background colour of the circle underneath.

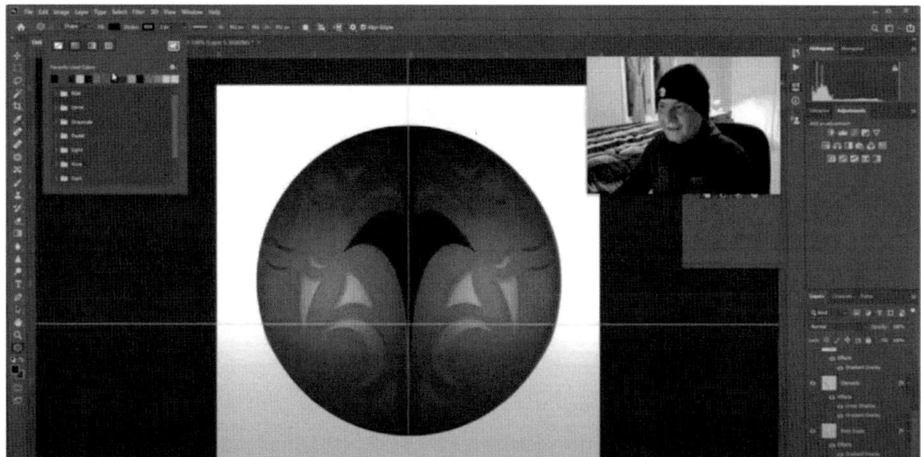

You can delete the duplicate and try more things. To add texture, use Control + A and Control + C to copy the texture from another canvas:

Paste it to the main canvas with Control + V:

Hit Control + T and drag it over and resize it:

Right click on the layer and hit "clipping mask"

The clipping mask takes the wood texture into the eagle. To add the abalone texture to the eyes, use the same process. Control + A and Control + C.

Hit Control + V to paste it onto the canvas.

Match it to the size:

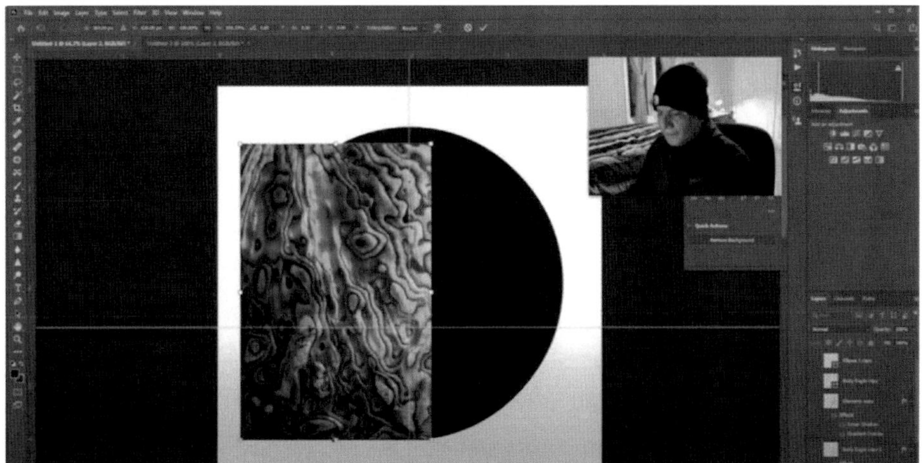

Right click on the layer you want to add it to and create clipping mask:

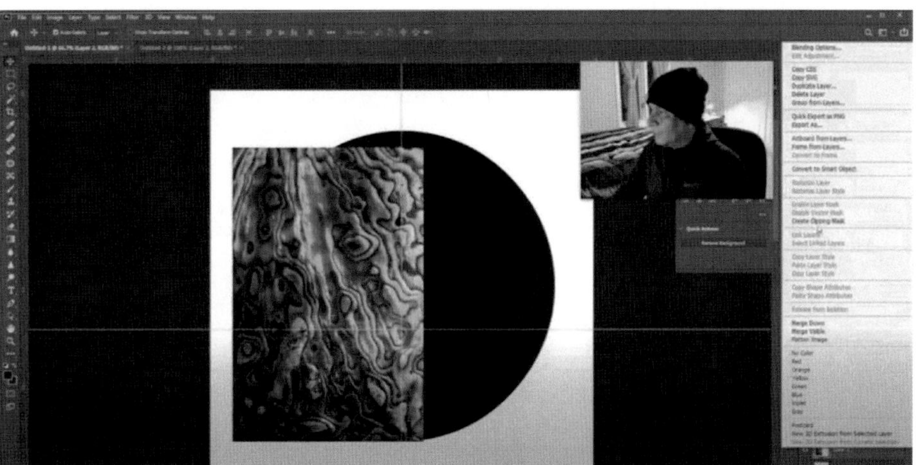

That will apply the texture to the layer:

You can use any texture you want, the possibilities are endless. Go back to the blending options and add the inner shadow:

Add shading to the body in blending options:

Try satin to add a different effect:

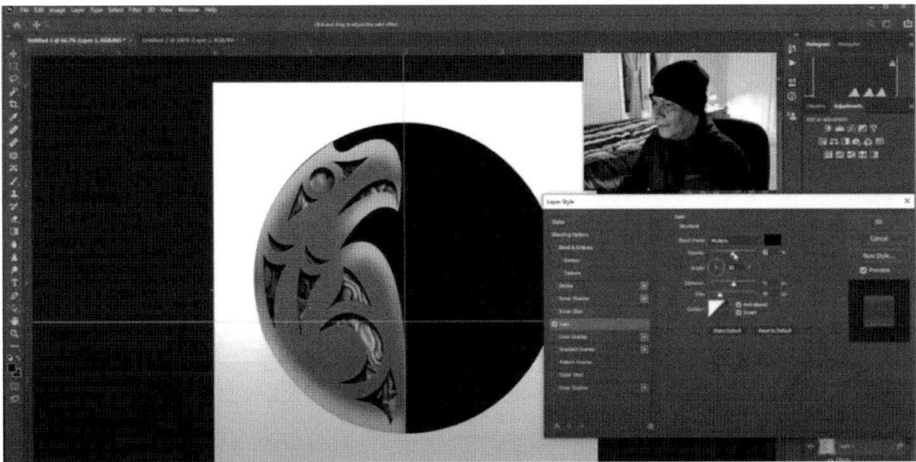

Invert the effect so it's the outline:

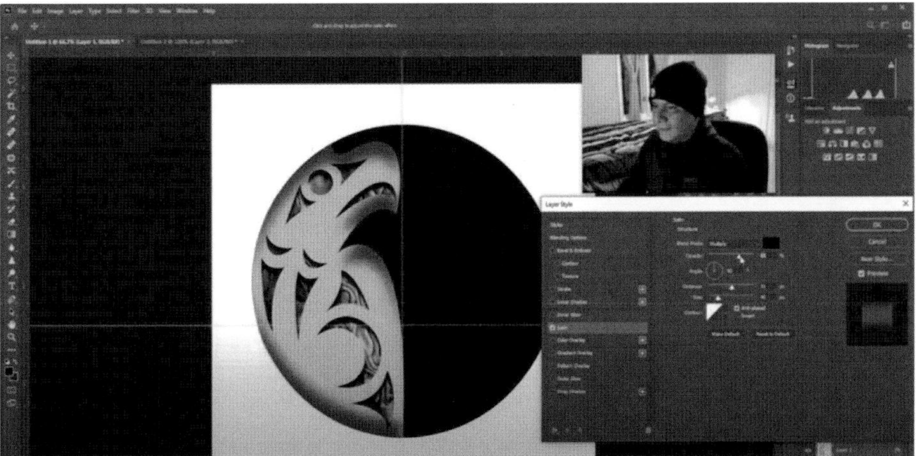

Use Control + J and Control + T to duplicate the image again.

If you want to add a texture to the circle behind use Control + V:

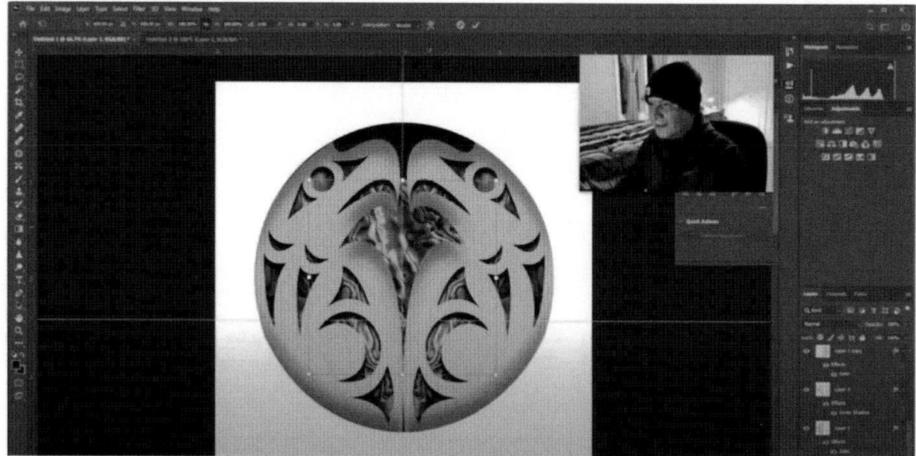

Stretch it to the right size:

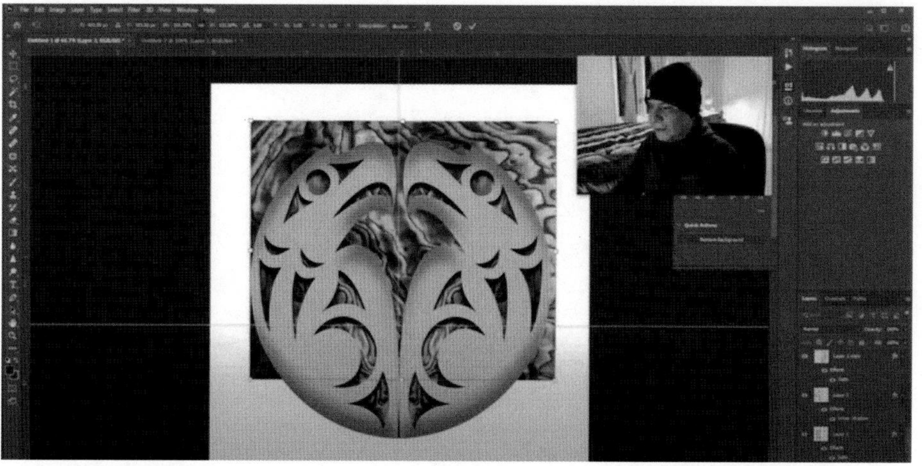

Make a clipping mask for the circle:

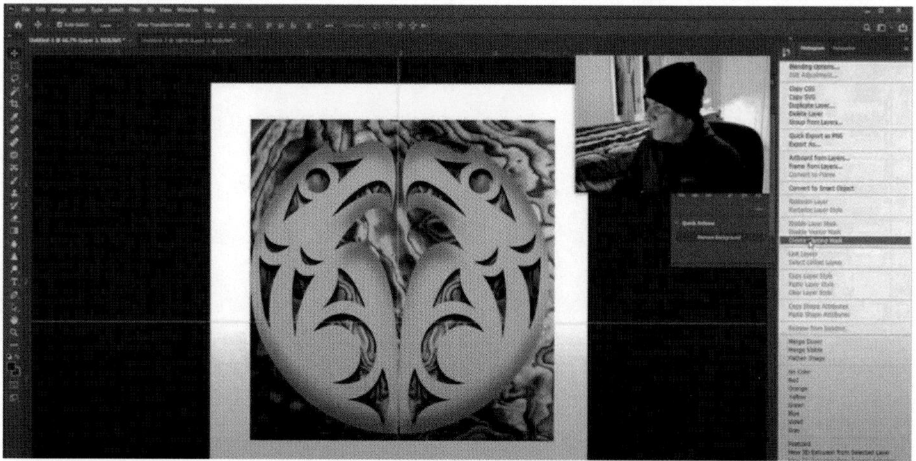

The texture will then be neatly applied:

Use Control + T to make a duplicate of the outer circle and expand it to create a border:

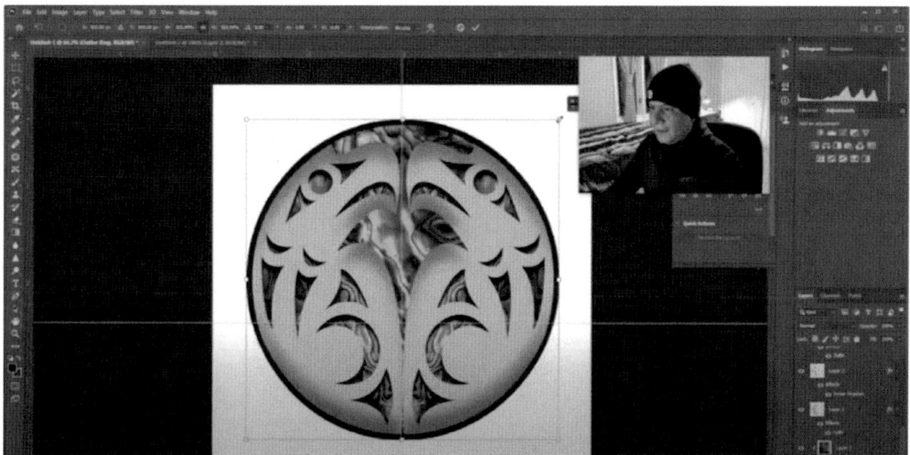

You can change the colour of the background:

If you stick with a white background, here's the final product:

With all those lessons, you can make some creative graphic art for yourself. What will you make?

POLITICS WITH NANCY KARETAK-LINDELL

Nancy Karetak-Lindell is the President of the Inuit Circumpolar Council Canada and was the first Member of Parliament for the new riding of Nunavut in 1997. She was re-elected twice, serving as Minister of Natural Resources, the Chair of the Standing Committee on Aboriginal Affairs and Northern Development, and a member of the Standing Committee on Fisheries and Oceans over her 11 years as MP. Her incredible achievements belie the challenges of her early years spent in the residential school system.

Ms. Karetak-Lindell was born and raised in the small, close-knit community of Arviat (renamed for a period under colonialism as Eskimo Point) during the 1950s and 60s. The community's residential school only went to grade eight, so at the age of 14 she was forced to attend a high school in Yellowknife, 1,000 km away from home.

Luckily, the young Nancy loved learning, and because there were so few high school graduates in her community, she was determined to achieve that goal. But her first year in Yellowknife was especially lonely, as the government at that time did not allow the students to go home for any holidays or winter break. "That was really tough. You went to school in September and you went home in June." Such was just one of the many cruel indignities the residential school system imposed on children and their families.

After two years in Yellowknife, Nancy's uncle encouraged her to join him in Ottawa to complete her high school education. While it was a huge opportunity for a girl from a tiny Arctic community to live somewhere as big and busy as Ottawa, it was another 1,200 km from home. "By the time I finished high school, I'd been away going on seven years." Nancy needed to reconnect, and so she spent a year back in Arviat working at the Inuit Cultural Institute. But the lure of higher education kept pulling at her, so Nancy returned to Ottawa for another year of schooling (Ontario offered a post-graduation Grade 13 for those who wanted to go on to university). And then she attended Trent University. "I really felt that I hadn't completed what I should complete, so I went back .... so I could accomplish something not many Inuit had opportunities to do. And that led me to believe that whatever I chose to do, I had to be disciplined."

After graduating, Nancy returned to Arviat to marry and start her family. She had planned to quietly settle down, but her extraordinary experiences made her desirable to the community leaders. "We tend to underestimate ourselves," she admits. "I kept telling people, 'I don't know how to do that, I've never been a committee member. I've never been a councillor.'" But one of the community elders encouraged her to recognize everything she had to offer. "He said to me, 'You have a different perspective, you've been outside our community, you've graduated, you've had to go through the schooling system.'" He encouraged her to sit on an education committee, which she enjoyed so much, she ran for the next election. And won. And went on to run and win more and greater positions within her larger community, leading all the way to being the federal representative of the entire territory, as Member of Parliament for Nunavut.

Ms. Karetak-Lindell acknowledges that her parents inspired her with their community involvement, but also through the harsh experiences they suffered under a system that aimed to suppress the Indigenous culture. "They were told where to send their children to school. They were told what language their children are going to learn. They really had no say.... My mother was always helping women and being a voice for them...and I realized that I [could] become a voice for those people that did not have a voice."

As the Member of Parliament for Nunavut, Ms. Karetak-Lindell served three terms, and visited every community in the territory to ensure she properly represented the entire population of that 1.9 million square kilometre area.

Ms. Karetak-Liddell understands first hand that in order to achieve and succeed, you need to stay determined. She sees a great message for her children, her grandchildren, and for young people today, in the symbol of her great territory: "The symbol for the Nunavut Government is a polar bear moving forward, but looking back, and there's a North Star leading his way. We have to find a way to lead ourselves somewhere. But again, that choice is up to us. We have to want to do it. No matter how much people support us, we have to believe in ourselves and say, 'I want to accomplish something!'"

MUSIC INDUSTRY BASICS

Caid Jones

View the videos in this series online! Scan the QR code, or visit http://www.tigurl.org/musicbasics

Caid Jones is an Indigenous/Irish recording artist out of Winnipeg Manitoba, Canada. He is the Co-Founder and Creative director for PayAttention Records. He specializes in Hip-Hop, R&B, audio production and is passionate about environmental/ social justice.

In this series, you will gain the knowledge you need for if you want to get started in the music industry with audio production, beat production, hip hop, or R and B.

LESSON 1: EQUIPMENT

We'll start by looking at Caid's setup. He has his Akai MPK Mini:

He's also got his audio interface:

And a Digital Audio Workstation (DAW), which is where you're going to record into, what you're going to produce out of and what you're going to export from to create your songs. Caid uses Reason but there are other kinds like LogicPro, FruityLoops, ProTools and Audacity.

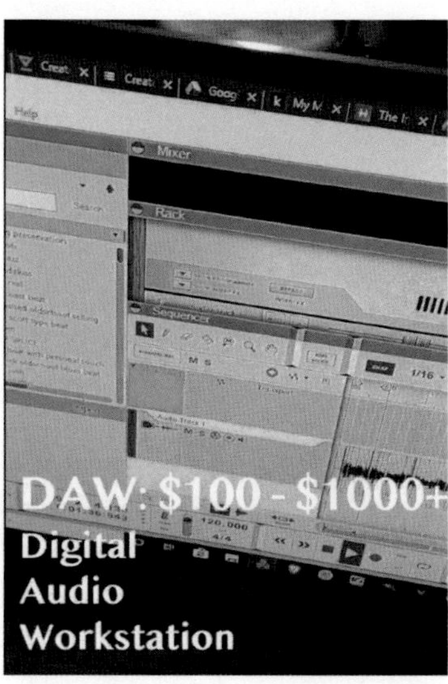

Microphone:

The biggest investments will be your laptop, your Digital Audio workstation and your microphone. You can use entry-level products to start out and upgrade as you go. Get what you need and get ready to get started!

LESSON 2: DISTRIBUTION AND PUBLISHING

Now that you have equipment, you can start making music. These are some things for you to know.

Distribution:
Your distributors are going to make sure that music's getting out to the world by sending it to iTunes and Spotify for a small fee. If you go and sign up for certain distributors, there's a lot of resources out there, like SOCAN, Distrokid, Songtrust, Tunecore, CD Baby. Some of these will do both distribution and publishing.

Publishing:
Your publishing is going to make sure that you get paid for those. There's two different types of royalties for publishing. Those are your mechanical royalties and your performance royalties. Publishing will just make sure that you get paid every time somebody streams your song, every time a radio station plays it, every time somebody uses it.

Copyright:
Every time you create a song, you own a copyright. If you create the instrumental and the lyrics and own the master recording, you own the copyright and you don't have to register it anywhere. If you do a feature with somebody, a producer on a beat, automatically, unless decided otherwise, that would be split 50% - 50% between the composer and the songwriter.

Licensing:
You own your song unless you decide to license it or give it out otherwise. You give your distributors a license to put your music out on streaming services.

Tools for Producers:
Beatstars and Splice are tools you can use to post and license beats, find royalty-free sounds and samples. They will charge a monthly fee which isn't usually much but as an independent artist it's up to you which service you choose.

Once you have the right tools you need the right people. Make sure you're surrounding yourself with good like-minded people with vision to help you learn the things that you need to learn to go forward.

LESSON 3: YOUR TEAM

"You can't build a good vision without good people around you and it won't succeed if everybody's arguing and nobody's on the same page."

Many people starting out wonder if they need a manager, an accountant or a publicist. The truth is you don't need people in those roles when you are starting out, but you do need to be able to know about the things they do. You can research and do them yourself at first.

If you want to earn an income off of your music, when you're building a team you need people that:

- fit your vision
- are like you
- are going to bring you up
- have better skills than you
- are doing more than you
- complement your weaknesses
- criticize your strengths even

This will help you grow and understand:

- your tendencies
- who you are
- what you need to work on

You might not need an accountant, a publicist or a manager, you do need to know:

- your peers
- who you surround yourself with

- Who's bringing up your music and your career
- your demographic
- Yourself
- who you're sending your music out to
- who's listening to your music
- what kind of music you make
- who you want to try and market that music to.

"You need to have confidence in your experimentation at this basic level. This is the time when you surround yourself with people who are challenging you. When you challenge yourself, when you build your skills, when you go and research, when you're gathering all these things at the basic level, this will contribute to a good career down the line, but you have to focus on the basics first."

"You can't run without walking. You can't walk without crawling, you can't bike without training wheels at first. You don't need to go and find all of these people at once. Go find people that are building the community. Go find people that are contributing to artistic growth, who want to collaborate."

Collaborations
You always want to collaborate with different artists that are challenging you in different artists that are growing, that fit your vision, and align with your priorities. Networking is super key with getting to know people.

With the right equipment and the right people, you can build the career of your dreams! Now go make music and magic!

LESSON 4: THE THREE PILLARS THAT EVERY ARTIST STARTING OUT SHOULD KNOW

"If you combine all three of these pillars as an independent artist, you are doing what you should be doing. They're very important for every artist."

Work ethic, networking, content are the three pillars every artist starting out should know (and every artist who is deep in their career should know and continue to follow.)

Work Ethic
There are so many artists out there who want to get their music out so it's important you're putting in lots of work and effort towards it. It's a very big playing field right now and that's great for all young artists who want to start out.

With access to the web and all these different resources, so many people want to get into it, which is great. Don't let it discourage you from putting in work and hours. Make sure that the fans know why your product is important and put in the hours towards the product.

If you're just expressing, being authentic, releasing the music, and doing it consistently, you'll find people out there who like it, community groups, people who will enjoy your music if you continue doing it.

Content

You want to be consistent with releasing content as an independent artist, and you want to be showing people what you're up to and what you're doing. This will contribute to your growth as an attribute and people will be able to see your story and connect with you.

Continue releasing content and don't be afraid of people who don't enjoy it because there will be people who do enjoy it if you're being authentic, being yourself and doing what you should be on an independent level.

Networking

If you're an independent artist, any level of professional level and want to advance anywhere you'll want to network. Through networking you'll get to share your music, your personality, your skill and it will contribute to your growth in a lot of ways.

Community grows in so many ways. You never know who can help you, who can value you in a relationship or how you can value them and what you can work on together. Networking helps get your name out, shows people you're involved and that you're serious about it.

FIRST NATION LEADERSHIP WITH CHIEF CHRISTOPHER DERICKSON

Chief Christopher Derickson is Syilx and serves as the Ilmixem (Chief) of the Westbank First Nation. As a child, he lived in the cities of Vancouver and Calgary, but moved back at age 11 to become known as "one of the worst kids on the reserve." His is an inspirational journey from that troubled youth to the position of Chief (as well as lecturer at Simon Fraser University and the University of Arizona, founder of an Indigenous community planning organization, Chair of the Okanogan College Board, member of the All Nations Trust Company, and more).

When Chief Derickson and his family returned to their reserve, he was faced with the extreme contrast between their previous middle class suburban life and the poverty of the reserve. "There was a noticeable cultural shift .... And unfortunately, just like most reserves across Canada, we have a number of social issues within our community. It was a lot worse when I was a kid....Then, there was really nothing for the young people."

Being an Indigenous teen learning about his own people "from the perspective of the colonizers" was infuriating to the young Christopher. "I remember distinctly that it awoke some sort of anger in me. A very angry child, I got in a lot of fights at school." By the time he was 14, Christopher was smoking, drinking, and doing drugs. And at 17, he unexpectedly became a father.

"I remember in the hospital, holding my baby boy in my arms, who was literally the size of a baseball cap, and thinking to myself, 'I don't want this child to be anything like the person I am today. It was a wake-up call for me."

As Christopher took one path to clean himself up, many of his friends went in the opposite direction, tragically including his young son's mom. "I lost a lot of friends to drugs, alcohol, gang initiations that went sideways. Lost a lot of friends, even lost the mother of my son. She passed away when he was only four or five years old from a drug overdose."

The challenges of being a young single father were made more difficult for Christopher as he attempted to improve his education. "Took me an extra two years to graduate high school, kept failing math class. I went to university from there, and promptly almost got kicked out, was put on academic probation twice." Christopher recognized the fault was not with him, but with the system he had grown up in. "I wasn't ready for [university] because nobody had taught me. I didn't know about the skills you needed to study, to write papers, to speak disciplined in that way. I had never done things like that in my life. So I ended up dropping out."

However, it was his son who again gave Christopher the strength to persevere. "We named him Justin, because of that connotation [with] justice. I wanted justice for my son. It wasn't his choice to come into this world to teenage characters....and I felt it was my job to bring a sense of justice to his life. I am just so grateful that I was able to find that purpose."

He studied for a master's degree in Indigenous Planning, received a law degree from UBC, and an MBA from Simon Fraser University. "Three degrees later, I'm still not satisfied," he admits. "I'm still waiting for the opportunity to go back and do a doctorate."

Today, Chief Derickson is proud to say that the "young and dynamic council that I serve with [is] actually the most educated council in the history of Westbank First Nation." Chief Derickson credits his parents for that. "The example that I had growing up, was that community involvement was just expected. A part of your life." His father, especially, was passionate about community politics, though he was "what you might call a dissident...a heavy critic of the Chief and Council." This meant "loud debates around the kitchen table."

But that passion inspired the way in which Chief Derickson, who goes by the term Ilmixem, has chosen to serve: "Ilmixem is the term in our language for chief, and it actually paints a picture of bringing strands and a rope together and coiling those strands on top of itself; like coiling a rope to make a tower. If you can picture that, that's what it means. To bring people together and build something beautiful together, and intricate and delicate out of. So I see my role as bringing people together and using their strengths."

"There is a strong need in our communities for professionals who understand our people. And we've relied far too long — as Indigenous people — on outside consultants, outside advice. And I truly believe that the answers our community requires, they're within our people. So if you're going to leave, some of you will go out, I'm sure, find careers out in the world off-reserve. And I think that's a noble path to take. But for some of you, you're going to have a strong call back to your community and you may look and think there's not a lot of opportunity there, you might see the challenges. But at some point in your life, you have to realize that's what life's about, is meeting these challenges head-on and finding the solutions. And who better to solve those problems for our people than ourselves?"

FISH SKIN TANNING AT HOME

Amber Sandy

View the videos in this series online! Scan the QR code, or visit http://www.tigurl.org/fishskin

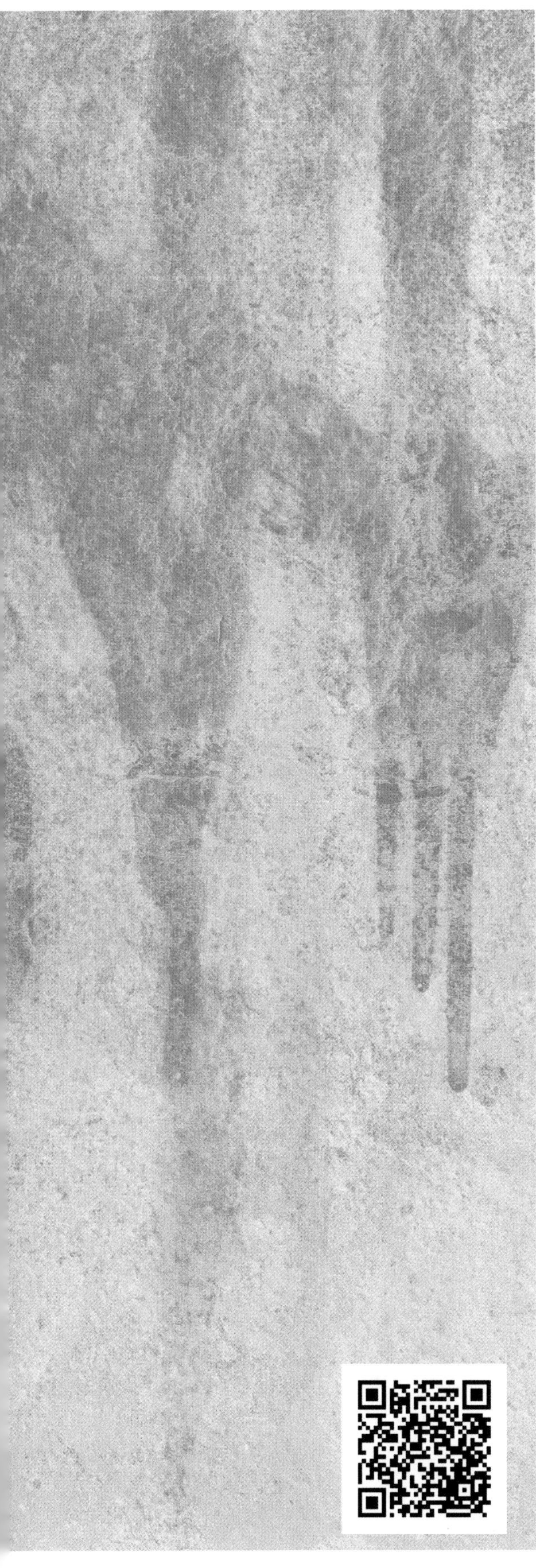

A member of Neyaashiinigmiing First Nation, Amber is an artist and advocate for Indigenous Science! Her work focuses on integrating Indigenous and western science in her approach to conservation, environmental science and education.

"Fish skin tanning at home [is] really fun and really easy to do."

In this lesson, you'll see how Amber tans fish skins to make leather, to use for art or all sorts of projects. In Amber's Create to Learn tutorial she tans perch skins donated by some ice fishermen who didn't need them. This tutorial is updating using the tea method which she has recently developed and recommends.

What you need

- Fish skin, any kind will work. Raw skins can be frozen until ready to use!
- Black tea bags
- Dish soap
- Spoon and butterknife
- Salt
- Glass jar/container
- Bowl
- Tea towel
- Oil (any kind works including olive, vegetable, neatsfoot, margarine and more!)

Tip: Take fresh fish skins and package them in-between parchment paper or wax paper for easy freezing. That way, you can grab as many as you want to use at a time.

SOURCING FISH SKINS

To source your skins, think sustainably. If you are planning on cooking fish for dinner, you can skin the fish before you cook it.

I have friends and family who go fishing save their skins for me. This is a great way to get a variety of local species.

You can try asking local fishmongers for their discarded fish skin, I have had a lot of luck with local sushi restaurants who have an abundance of salmon skin that gets thrown out.

Freeze your skins right away until the day you will tan them. If you have lots, sorting them is nice so you can take as many as you want, otherwise toss them in a bag and freeze!

It is important to remember that fish skins need to always remain cold!

STEP ONE: MAKE YOUR TEA

Bring a pot of water to boil, put 5 black tea bags and a spoon of salt (salt is openly needed on day 1) in and let cool to room temperature

Each day you will refresh your tea with a new batch and we will slowly increase the amount of tea each day.

Day 1: 5 tea bags
Day 2: 10 tea bags
Day 3: 15 tea bags
Day 4-6+: 20 tea bags

STEP TWO: FLESHING AND SCALING

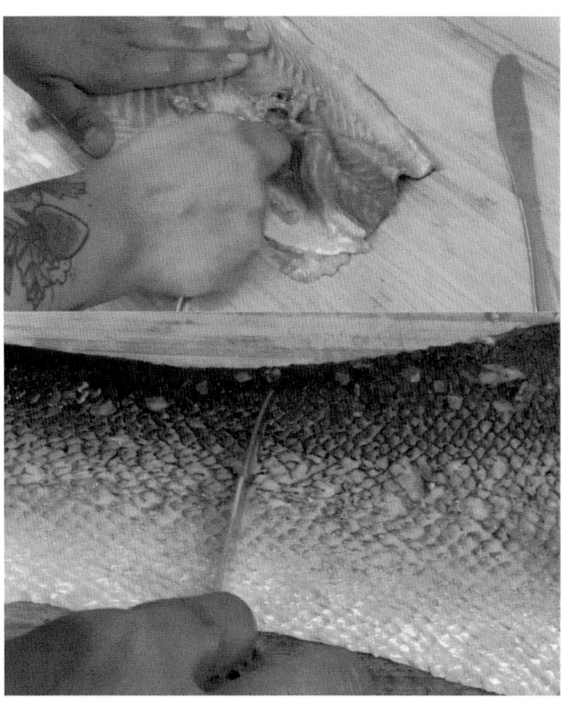

Using your spoon, flesh out the inside of the skin. Ensure that you get as much of the thin, silvery parts on the skin off as possible. Flip over the skin and use the backside of your butterknife to scrape off the scales.

Scrape from tail to head and be gentle to keep the scale pockets intact, as they give fish leather it's beautiful texture!

Step Three: Washing

Fill your bowl with COLD water and dish soap, give your skins a good wash to get any excess oils off of them. This will better allow the tannins in the tea to penetrate the skin.

It is very important to make sure your skins only come into contact with cool water/tea. They will begin to disintegrate when submerged in warm/hot water.

STEP FOUR: TANNING

When your tea has cooled completely, transfer it to your glass jar and your skins are ready to go into the tea. Stir the tea often! Every time I walk by my jar I give it a stir, this will help to evenly tan the skins. The more they are agitated, the quicker they tan. Your tea can stay out and will not go bad because you will be changing it each day, keeping it in a cool place out of direct sunlight.

Change your tea each day according to the chart in the tea section. Stir, stir, stir! At day 4, snip a little corner off your skin to check how it's doing. If it's still white on the inside it's not done tanning, and you can keep going and make a stronger tea if needed. When the skin is the same colour throughout, it is finished being tanned! Give or take about 6 days and it will be tanned!

STEP FIVE: OILING, STRETCHING AND DRYING

Wash your skin really well with cold water and dish soap to get any excess tannins of the skin. Wring out your skin in a tea towel to take out as much moisture as possible. Coat your skin with the oil of your choice, and work that oil into the skin. Using your hands and any other tools you want to try, stretch the skin and continue to work it as it dries.

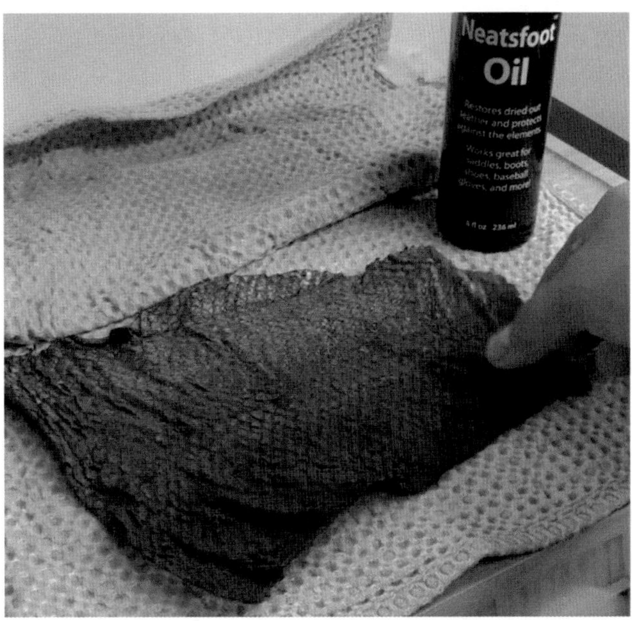

FINAL STEPS

When all of the oil feels absorbed in the skin, introduce more for a second time. Continue working the skin. If it dries while not being worked, it will dry stiff! Once your skin is dry, you can coat it with a leather conditioner or beeswax to shine it up if you wish. Now you have some beautiful, handmade leather that you can make anything you would make with leather!

Manufactured by Amazon.ca
Bolton, ON